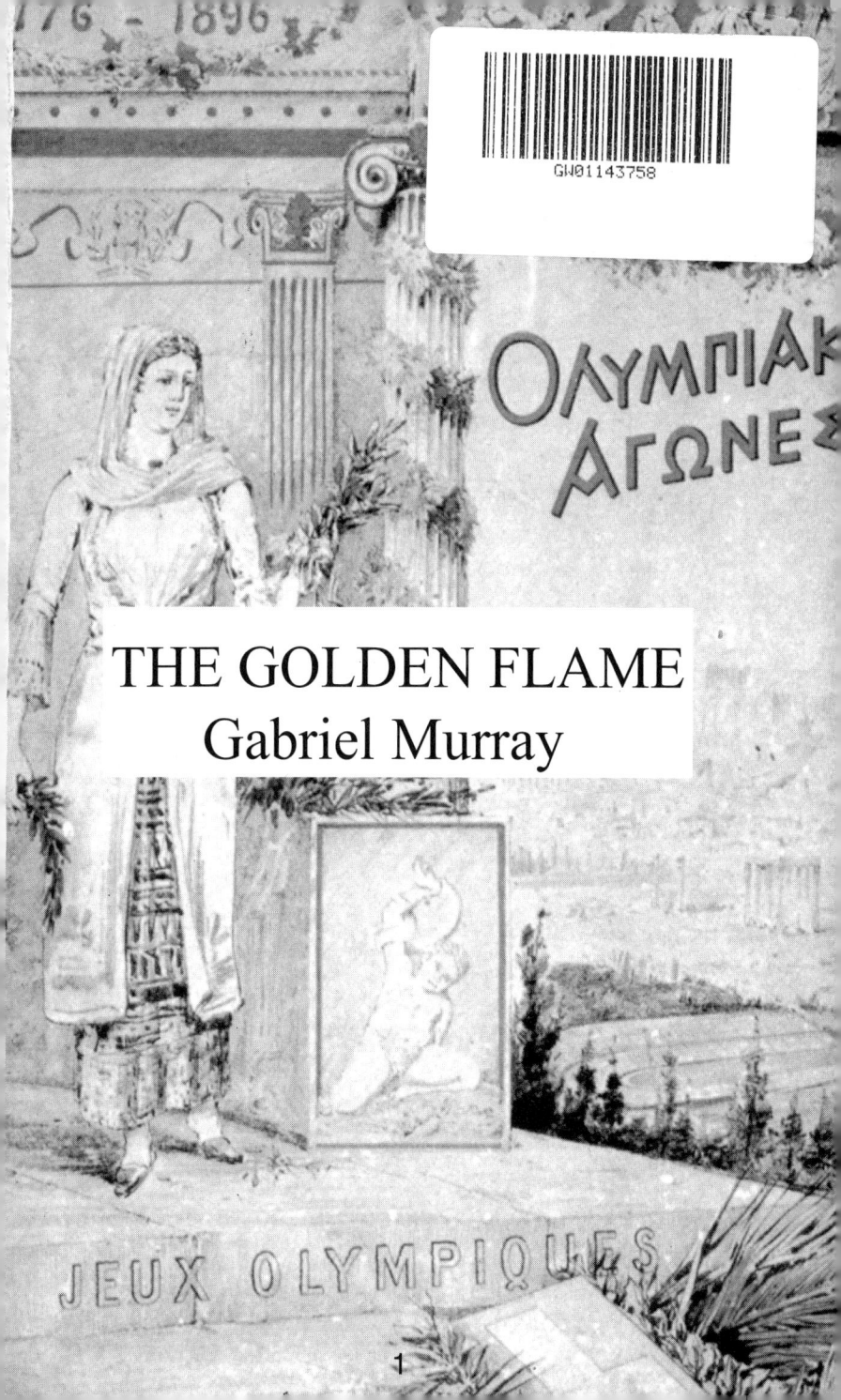

THE GOLDEN FLAME
Gabriel Murray

The GOLDEN FLAME

To Dad,
Keep the flame burning — 28/03/06
Gabriel

NIKE, GODDESS OF VICTORY.

The most important thing in the Olympic Games is

not to win but to take part, just as the most important

thing in life is not the triumph but the struggle

The essential thing is not to have conquered

but have fought well.

ATHENS 1896

*Keep watch on the sacred flame, and remember the sun kindled
fire that has come to you from Olympia .
Guard it jealously in the debths of your being.*

*Pierre De Coubertin
1863-1937*

NIKE, GODDESS OF VICTORY.

Also by Gabriel Murray

Novels
Dreams of Deliverance
The Zhivago File

Screenplays
Goddess
Stoker
The Boys are Back in Town
Whisky in the Jar
The File on the Tsar.
Schiele and Klimpt
Messiah

Non Fiction
Proust and Visconti
The Countess of Desart

For My Brother James

Published by Ailesbury Publications, Ltd.
Molyneux House,
Bride Street,
Dublin 8

© Gabriel Murray

E mail: atthegoldenflame@yahoo.co.uk

First published in Ireland by Ailsbury Publications Ltd 2004.
Gabriel Murray asserts the moral right to be identified as the author of this work.

A catalogue record of the book is available
from
The British Library.

ISBN. 0-9548062-1-2

Printed and bound in England by Bath Books.
All rights reserved.
No part of this publication
may be reproduced, stored in a retrieval syste or
transmitted in any form or by any means, electronic,
photocopying, recording or otherwise, without the
prior written permission of the publishers

About the Author

Gabriel Murray was born in Ireland. He has written a number of novels and screenplays on biographical and historical subjects; "Dreams of Deliverance," about the Falasha Black Jews of Ethiopia and their escape from persecution; "The Zhivago File," based on the love story between Olga Invanskoya and Boris Pasternak and their subsequent battle to publish Doctor Zhivago.
He has adapted two books by Anthony Summers to screenplay; "Goddess, The Secret Lives of Marlyn Monroe" and "The Last Tsar," based on the Sokolov Investigations which dealt with the murder of Tsar Nicholas 11 and the "Anastasia mystery."

He has written a number of other screenplays on Irish subjects, notably "Stoker," the Irishman who wrote "Dracula," and "The Boys are Back in Town" about the birth of Irish Rock featuring the story of Phil Lynott. Bono and Bob Geldof. Another screenplay is based on Handel's first performance of the Messiah in 17th century Dublin.

Academic research has involved him in researching the lost history of The Countess of Desart, the Jewish Senator in the Irish Government who gave all her wealth to social causes in Ireland. Another project is a research on Proust and Visconti's forgotten screenplay of "Remberance of Things Past.

"I knew prejudice even after I became a Olympic champion. I'd gone over there and defiled (Hitler) a man who changed the shape of the world but that didn't matter, I still had to sit in the back of the bus. Thankfully things began to change with Doctor Martin Luther King and others even before him. In the 1930's black people had no image they could relate to. Then along came two people, Joe Louis and Jesse Owens. Because of what we did, cracks began to appear in the door. It was Doctor King who opened the book of justice, I think-your ideas being passed from father to son.

That's immortality, .The road to the Olympics does not lead to any particular country or within us. It goes far beyond Moscow or ancient Greece or Nazi Germany. The road to the Olympics leads, in the end,, to the best within us."

Jesse Owens

The Olympic Revival

Athens 1896

THE OLYMPIC REVIVAL

Irish author Gabriel Murray tells the story of the revival and the first Irish americqn Olympic Team,in his book "The Golden Flame"

Where did the spark for the Olympic revival begin? Its founder, Frenchman Baron, Pierre de Coubertin, followed a long established Olympic trail to recreate the ancient Olympics. Long before de Coubertin arrived in Athens, there was a Greek Olympic revival in progress, created by Evanghelos Zappas, a wealthy Greek living in Romania. It was King Otto, King of the Hellenes, who first suggested the idea in 1837. In 1854, Greek writer Soutsos wrote an article suggesting the revival of the games. Zappas read this article and became enthusiastic. He engaged architects and builders and invested large sums of money in the project which resulted in the erection of The Zappieon and the rebuilding of the ancient stadium.

The first Greek Olympic revival actually occurred in 1859 in Freedom Square, Athens. Zappas died in 1865 leaving a fortune to the games. His will stipulated that the games were to be held every four years and that the stadium should continue to be rebuilt. There were two further Olympics after Zappas' death in 1875. The seed of the Olympic idea also had roots in England and Ireland. In the village of Much Wenlock in Shropshire, Dr William Penny Brookes founded the Much Wenlock Olympic Society in 1850, nine years before the Zappian games. The King of Greece regularly corresponded with Brookes, sending him cups and medals as rewards for the victors. Brookes returned his offerings by awarding prizes to the Zappian Games. In Ireland, the Tailteann games had close similarities with the ancient Olympics. Both games observed the sacred truce between the Celts and the Greeks, dating from around 600BC.

De Coubertin visited Ireland in 1890 shortly after the revival of the Tailteann and Gaelic games. It took this young French aristocrat to make the international connections and establish the games. In 1890 he met with Brookes at Much Wenlock and was inspired by his ideal, organising the Olympic Congress in Paris at the Sorbonne in 1894. There he whipped up international support. It was at this conference that the first meeting of the International Olympic Committee occurred and it was decided that the games be revived in Athens in 1896. Demetrios Vikelas, a Greek living in Paris, was president of the games.

It was only after this conference that the Greek government was consulted and it was for this reason that de Coubertin visited Greece in 1895. Tricoupis, the prime minister, turned down the project and it was only due to Prince Constantine's and the King's support that the idea gained credibility in Greece. Constantine formed a 12 person committee known as the 12 apostles to help raise funds throughout Greece, but only a small amount was raised. However, Prince Constantine contacted the wealthiest man in Greece, millionaire Georgios Averoff, who lived in Alexandria in Egypt. It was on meeting de Coubertin that he agreed to bankroll the entire project and pay for the final reconstruction of the stadium located in central Athens. De Coubertin announced the world which created a fever of international support throughout Greece.

The games began on Easter Sunday 1896, attended by 100,000 people, after a break of 1,504 years. The American team swept the field, winning all the track events , The Irish American team led by Captain Robert Garrett, a Harvard graduate, were victors of all the track events, becoming the world's first modern Olympians. Irishman, James Connolly, of the Boston Athletic Club, led the field. Loues, a poor Greek Shepherd, won the marathon, a race not run for over 2000 years. He became a hero throughout Greece.

"The book captures the heroic struggle of the first Irish American Olympic athletes and their battle to attend the Athens Games and the great and the good they met along the way to Olympic fame."

Review. European Bookseller

The Lost History of the Olympic Games

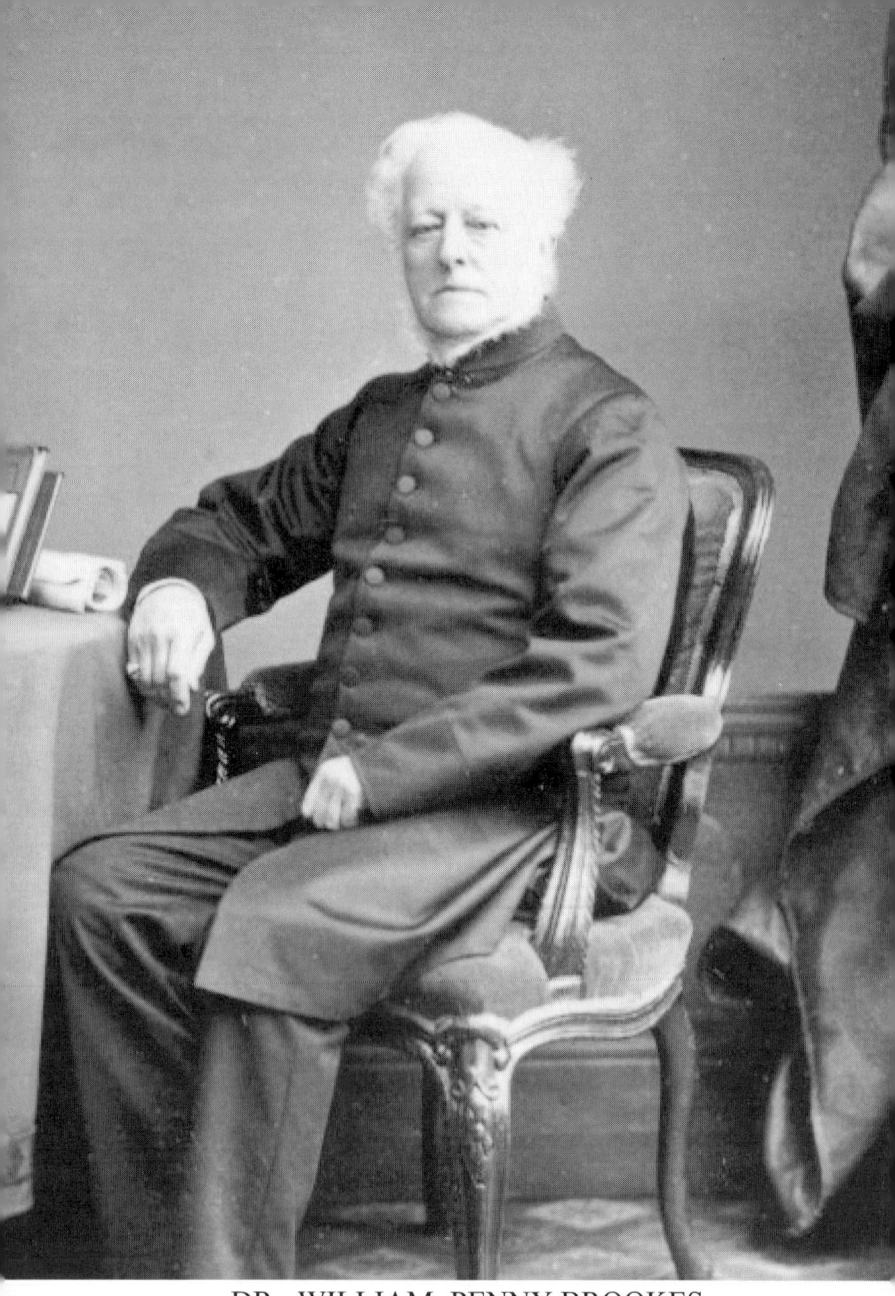

DR . WILLIAM PENNY BROOKES
Founder of the Much Wenlock Olympian Society
He inspired De Coubertin to revive the Olympic Games.

Much Wenlock lays claim to its Olympic birthright.

This tiny Shropshire town of Much Wenlock reckons itself to be the true cradle of the modern Olympic movement for it has been running games modelled on those of classical Greece since 1890. The opening ceremony of this year's festival revolved around the launch of a romantic fictionalised novel about the Olympic movement titled the Golden Flame.

The more publicised Olympic flame arrives amid unprecedented hype in Atlanta tomorrow to set off the celebrations for the hundredth anniversary of the Olympic Games. There will be much talk of Baron Pierre de Coubertin, honoured by history as the self- styled founding father of the Olympics but in Much Wenlock they know better. They have their own local hero, a doctor named William Penny Brookes, who was ahead of de Coubertin by almost half a century in reviving the ancient Olympiad. Not only that, as his biographer, Helen Cromarty, is eager to point out, he met de Coubertin and passed on like a relay torch his detailed blueprint for the modern Olympic Games.

The French aristocrat grabbed the project with enthusiasm, initially acknowledging his debt to the Englishman. In 1890 he wrote: "If the Olympic Games, which modern Greece has not been able to revive, still survive today, it is not to a Greek that we are indebted, but rather to Doctor W.P. Brookes."

But by the time the games were up and running, de Coubertin was apparently suffering an Olympian loss of memory, and taking all the credit for the revival for himself. There was not a mention of Brookes as the baron dashed off articles such as "Why I revived the Olympic Games." If rip-offs had been in the Olympics, this one would have carried off the gold.

The beamed bar of the Raven Hotel, an old coaching inn in Much Wenlock, on an English July afternoon is about as far away from the cauldron of the Olympic stadium as you can get. But it was there, in the late summer of 1890, that de Coubertin dined with the remarkable Doctor Brookes. He was a local G. P. a reformer and dreamer who, in 1850, founded the Much Wenlock Olympian Society whose goals were to develop the physical and intellectual strengths of the inhabitants of the town and neighbourhood of Wenlock and especially the Working Classes.

Dr Brookes clearly believed that healthy exercise would keep men off the streets and out of the pubs. He took as his inspiration and model the ancient Olympics and although his first attempts were a mixture of old country sports-from cricket and acrobatics to athletics, there was a certain pageantry which was certainly Greek in style.

He paraded banners with Greek inscriptions, and winners were honoured with laurel branches and medal bearing a representation of Nike- the Greek goddess of victory. Brookes also built up strong Contacts with Greece and in 1877, he Greek King George 1, even donated a silver cup to be awarded to the winner of the pentathlon.

The effect of all this Olympic veneer made a deep impression on a young French aristocrat who was eager to pedal physical edcation to what he considered to be the desperate youth of his native France. De Coubertin liked the idea of the Olympic Festival so much that he hijacked it and went on to claim it as his own. It is not the winning that matters, as he old baron might have said, it is the taking the credit.

The remarkable double act of Doctor Brookes and de Coubertin is chronicled in great detail in The Golden Flame, launched by the Irish author, Gabriel Murray, at Much Wenlock. Murray concludes of de Coubertin, "It was in England that he discovered Greece. It was there that he learnt of Olympia and found the ideal of his life."

"The sun shone warmly on the grass track at Wenlock's Linden Fields at the weekend and the sight of spectators and competitors pick-nicking with their tea and sandwiches evoked a sporting era left way behind by the other Olympian Games. They sent their President, Juan Antonio Samaranch, to pay homage to Brookes and plant an oak tree in his memory. When asked why he has come to Much Wenlock, Samaranch replied, "Because this is where the Olympics all started."

John Bryant
Deputy Editor of The Times.London

The Philosophy of De Coubertin

Keep watch on the sacred flame, and
remember the sun kindled fire
that has come to you from Olympia.
Guard it jealously in the depths of your being

The struggles of history will continue but, little by little, knowledge will replace dangerous ignorance. Mutual understanding will soften unthinking hatred. Thus, the edifice at which I laboured for half a century will be strengthened. Remember the sun-kindled fire, which has come to you from Olympia to lighten our epoch. Guard it jealously in the depths of your being

The Olympic Games may be a potent, if indirect, factor in securing world peace. Wars break out because nations misunderstand each other. We shall not have peace until prejudices, which now separate the different races, are outlived. It is not visionary to look for similar benefactions in the future

If I look back, I see from the end to the beginning my life as a man. I have been performing the job of a scout. A scout is one who goes forward to find the right way and the clear path. I was not aware of this occupation. I had chosen a different one and several times tried to escape it, always in vain. I think I was made for no other. At all events and instictive and secret force makes me stay faithful to it."

However, it had its sorrows and setbacks. First of all, it implies solitude. There are hours when one feels terribly alone, as if lost in a dark forest or on a bare mountain top. At such moments one turns anxiously and longingly back. However, contact is found again. The scout returns to his tracks to impart his discovery, and check whether the crowd is indeed following in his footsteps. It is at that moment that he sometimes experiences keen disappointment. Yes, the crowd is following, but it has forgotten him. It credits others with the results of his labours, and he feels like a stranger amongst his fellows. His opinions are not listened to and his comments are not heeded. Disorientated and misunderstood, he starts to wish to be alone, and he goes off keener and more ambitious than ever, but with a painful sense of injustice in his heart.

The Games have often been criticised since then, and even violently attacked. Not everybody comprehends it; many speak of it without knowing anything about its origin or its purpose.

There are people who talk about the elimination of war; those who treat these people as Utopians are not wrong. But there are others who talk about the progressive diminution of the chances of war, and I don't see that as Utopian at all. What I mean is that on a basis conforming to modern life we are to establish a great and magnificent institution, the Olympic Games."

The mist... is thus a fleeting darkness, and on the other side we will all find the sun and blue sky again.

It is for you to keep the flag flying… Olympism is a school of moral nobility and purity."

Life is simple because the fight is simple. The good fighter steps forward, but never gives up. He yields but never quite quits. If he is faced with the impossible, he turns away and goes further... and even if everything falls down around him, despair does not enter him.

Life is beautiful because the fight is beautiful. Not the bloody fight, fruit of tyranny and evil passions, which is maintained by ignorance and routine ... But the holy fight of souls seeking truth, light and justice.

Tthe Olympic ideal was universal, and that no race or epoch can claim an exclusive monopoly to it.

Have faith in it. Put out your strength for it. Make its hopes your own.

When a man is going to leave his fruitful soil on which he has dwelt for many years, he will want, on his last day, to climb up to a high place whence he can see the horizon. There, musing on the future, he will worry over unfinished tasks. He will think of improvements which could be made and measured. None of you should be surprised that such should be my state of mind at the moment.

Times are still difficult; the dawn which is breaking is that of the aftermath of the storm, but towards midday the sky will brighten and the ruddy corn will once more burden the arms of the harvester. It is not midday, gentlemen. The days of history are long; let us be patient and keep confident.

Perhaps one will judge that these remarks are inspired by pride. But if I have a high opinion of and take great pride in the work that was given to me to accomplish, I recognize no merit in it for myself. Merit begins there where the individual, obliged to struggle against himself or against excessively disfavorable circumstances, wins victories over his own temperament and, as it is said, succeeds in subduing his fate. Favored by lot in many respects, sustained unceasingly in the face of my task by a kind of internal force from which it happened that I searched in vain to escape, I count no such victories to my credit.

# The Original Vision

What was De Coubertin's original vision? What were the qualities that made up the man'? Why did he set out on this great quest to revive the ancient Games'? The Golden Flame seeks to examine these issues, in the light of the forces working against the new Olympic movement. Has. De Coubertin's vision become lost, for a new generation'? What was the original philosophy'? Perhaps the Atlanta games will help us focus on the life of De Coubertin, who sacrificed everything in the pursuit of his ideals.

This book attempts to illuminate the life of the man, whose life story and beliefs have become lost among the academic files of sports history. What is the future of Olympism? Commercialism has made massive in roads on the original ideals of the Games. The great and noble vision of De Coubertin's Olympism has suffered under great pressures.

But this was not always the case; before Montreal and Berlin, there was a time when young men stood beneath the five-ringed flag and the sacred flame, believing in the purer ideals of Olympism. It was a time when nationalism, political gain and profit were monsters that did not erode this great vision. Athens was the re-birth of the ideal.

De Coubertin's story deserves to be told again, if only to inspire the youth of the world today to carry a new torch - to set if alight and to rekindle the 'Golden Flame' - and to discover for themselves that ancient Olympic spirit once more.

***

The Lost Heritage of Olympism

The history books tell us that the ancient games of Olympia were revived on Easter Sunday 1896.

But the true story is more complex. All across Europe 150 years ago, people were heartily sick of the Industrial Revolution which had brought great wealth for some but smoke-blackened misery and ruined health for millions.

There was a romantic longing for the clean limbed simplicity and fair play of the Olympian ideal.

In England it was fitting that Shropshire, the county which gave birth to the Industrial Revolution at Coalbrookdale, also played a part in re-kindling the Olympic torch.

The story is told in a new novel, The Golden Flame, weaving fact and fiction together as its real-life hero, Pierre De Coubertin, roams the world for inspiration to re-stage the games.

In Shropshire he met Dr William Penny Brookes who had founded the Shropshire Olympics in 1850 - 46 years before the Athens revival.

Brookes saw the games as "a last innocent attempt to stop England's decay". It was a decay he witnessed almost daily from his small cottage and yet another coffin was brought to the cemetery, marking yet another untimely death.

The games were his way of challenging the future by drawing on the past.

"The contestants wore medieval costume and carried Olympic banners with Greek inscriptions. The winners were presented with laurel crowns.

"The medals were stamped with the image of the Maltese Cross enclosed in a wreathed medallion. Some of the medals had the image of Nike, goddess of victory, inscribed on them."

It sounds like a village sports day with ideas above its station. In fact, the games at Much Wenlock attracted the interest of the King of Greece, who donated some of the medals.

The idea gathered strength. Brookes founded the Shropshire Olympic Society in 1861 and the National Olympian Association in 1865.

Brooke's dream was to re-launch the Olympic Games as a British national event. But by the time he met De Coubertin, he was 82 and his strength was failing.

As writer Gabriel Murray recalls: "These were held on the rolling plains of Wenlock, in a place known as the Linden Fields. Hundreds of people assembled beside a gaily coloured grandstand and marquee. There, the young mascot, Tom Yeats, sounded his trumpet mounted on a white horse and galloped across the open fields declaring the Games open. Tom was dressed in a 16th century costume, recalling the images from Arthurian legend."

Inspired by their meeting, Pierre De Coubertin took over Brooke's task. In January 1894 he wrote to all athletic associations urging a revival of the Olympic Games which had run from 776 BC until being suppressed by the Church in the 4th century AD.

The response to De Coubertin's idea was lukewarm but a congress was held in Paris five months later. A revival was unanimously agreed for 1896, after a gap of 1,504 years, with the honour of staging the event falling to Athens.

The games caught the world's imagination and have been held every four years ever since, apart from the 1916, 1940 and 1944; events which were cancelled because of the First and Second World Wars.

As Atlanta prepares to host the 100th anniversary Olympics, few of the millions of viewers around the world will have heard of Shropshire's unlikely role in reviving the ancient ideals of sportsmanship.

But the town has not. Nearly 150 years after the Brookes staged his first sports meeting, Shropshire Councillors have just agreed on a feasibility study to build a heritage centre in Much Wenlock, in memory of a doctor whose vision helped to change the world.

But the true story is more complex. All across Europe 150 years ago, people were heartily sick of the Industrial Revolution which had brought great wealth for some but smoke-blackened misery and ruined health for millions.

There was a romantic longing for the clean limbed simplicity and fair play of the Olympian ideal. In England it was fitting that Shropshire, the county which gave birth to the Industrial Revolution at Coalbrookdale, also played a part in re-kindling the Olympic torch.

The story is told in a new novel, "The Golden Flame," weaving fact and fiction together as its real-life hero. Pierre de Coubertin, roams the world for inspiration to re-stage the games.

In Shropshire he met Dr William Penny Brookes who had founded the Shropshire Olympics in 1850 - 46 years before the Athens revival.

Brookes saw the games as "a last innocent attempt to stop England's decay". It was a decay he witnessed almost daily from his small cottage and yet another coffin was brought to the cemetery, marking yet another untimely death.

The games were his way of challenging the future by drawing on the past.

"The contestants wore medieval costume and carried Olympic banners with Greek inscriptions. The winners were presented with laurel crowns.

"The medals were stamped with the image of the Maltese Cross enclosed in a wreathed medallion. Some of the medals had the image of Nike, goddess of victory, inscribed on them."

It sounds like a village sports day with ideas above its station. In fact, the games at Much Wenlock attracted the interest of the King of Greece, who donated some of the medals.

The idea gathered strength. Brookes founded the Shropshire Olympic Society in 1861 and the National Olympian Association in 1865.

Brooke's dream was to re-launch the Olympic Games as a British national event. But by the time he met De Coubertin, he was 82 and his strength was failing.

As writer Gabriel Murray recalls: "These were held on the rolling plains of Wenlock, in a place known as the Linden Fields. Hundreds of people assembled beside a gaily coloured grandstand and marquee. There, the young mascot, Tom Yeats, sounded his trumpet mounted on a white horse and galloped across the open fields declaring the Games open. Tom was dressed in a 16th century costume, recalling the images from

Arthurian Legend."

Inspired by their meeting, Pierre De Coubertin took over Brooke's task. In January 1894 he wrote to all athletic associations urging a revival of the Olympic Games which had run from 776 BC until being suppressed by the Church in the 4th century AD.

The response to De Coubertin's idea was lukewarm but a congress was held in Paris five months later. A revival was unanimously agreed for 1896, after a gap of 1,504 years, with the honour of staging the event falling to Athens.

The games caught the world's imagination and have been held every four years ever since, apart from the 1916, 1940 and 1944 events which were cancelled because of the First and Second World Wars.

As Atlanta prepares to host the 100th anniversary Olympics, few of the millions of viewers around the world will have heard of Shropshire's unlikely role in reviving the ancient ideals of sportsmanship.

But the town has not. Nearly 150 years after the Brookes staged his first sports meeting, Shropshire Councillors have just agreed on a feasibility study to build a heritage centre in Much Wenlock, in memory of a doctor whose vision helped to change the world.

Peter Rhodes

The First Olympic Hero

Boston Irishman

James Connolly

"Life at Harvard was all right, but not exactly thrilling; whereas a sailing across the wide Atlantic, through the Gibraltar Straits...and so to the port of Piraeus where Homer must have landed on his way to The First Olympic Hero
Boston Irishman Janes brendan Connollyhens-there was certainly a better way of passing what should be pleasant afternoons than trying to chamfer a block of cold steel with a chisel."

James Connolly

THE FIRST OLYMPIC HERO
JAMES BRENDAN CONOLLY

James Connolly was born in the predominately Irish area of South Boston on Saturday, November 25th, 1865. He was the son of Sean Connolly, later to be know in Boston as John, and Aine O'Donnell, both from Mainister on Inis Mor in the Aran Islands.He was introduced to the sea as early as seven years of age. In his autobiography, published in 1944.

"For as long as my father and mother knew, their people came of sea-faring stock. They were Aran Islands folk; islands that lie off the west coast of Ireland. It was rough coast and the Arnas are little isles, which was one reason why so many men of those isles took to the sea. The lack of arable land left the sea as their best chance of a living".

On his arrival in America, Connolly's father joined the Boston fishing fleet. His mother's brother, Jim O'Donnell, joined the American coast from Boston. Connolly made many voyages to the fishing grounds in the Newfoundland banks and on the north Atlantic.

He became a surveyor of inland waterways around Boston. In 1895, Connolly entered the Engineering School at Harvard University, Connolly's other love was athletics. He was recognised in Boston as an outstanding competitor in both the high jump and long jump.

The local newspapers in Boston carried news that there would be a revival of the Olympic Games at Athens the following year. This caught fired up Connolly .He heard that fellow Bostonians and Irishmen, including some from Harvard, were planning to make the trip to Greece, he decided to apply for leave from Harvard.

The Dean of Harvard- told him that he could go on one condition only: he could immediately resign from Harvard and, on his return, he could apply again for admission.

The Dean also added the chances of being re-admitted were remote. Conolly was beyond his athletic prime anyway, and there was no point in going.

Connolly had made his mind. He immediately walked out of Harvard.

They were joined by four students from Princeton along with nine Boston athletes on March 19th, 1896. Their new captain was Robert Garrett. Professor Sloane, who received the original American invitation from the I.O.C., also joined them. Connolly took a train from Boston to New York and on the the 20th day set sail for Naples. Ten days later they reached Naples.

Crossing Italy they reached the port at Brindisi, they sailed down the Adriatic to Corfu, then to the port of Patras and that was followed by a 10-hour train trip to Athens.Travelling north of Olympia and across the Gulf of Corinth.

News spread rapidly of the American arrival, they were given an extraordinary welcome by members of the organising committee of the first Olympic Games. A massive banquet was thrown for them by Prince Constantine at the Royal Palace.

The Americans believed that the opening day of the Games was April 18th, which would give them 12 days to prepare for their events. They Greek calendar however was twelve days ahead of the American calendar. They had no time to train. The games began the following day. Conolly was exhausted; after six thousand miles and sixteen days of travel, he had to compete immediately.

On Tuesday, April 7th, 1896, on page five, The Irish Times carried this agency report:

"Athens, Monday: The opening of the Olympic Games today is observed as a national festival, enthusiastic interest being taken in the sports. The day was opened with a Te Deum in the Cathedral at which members of the Royal Family and the Russian Grand Duke George were present. The Russian Prince and his finance Princess Marie were heartily cheered.

"The spectators at today's events are calculated to have numbered 18,000. The Royal Party arrived at three o'clock. They were met in the centre of the arena by the Crown Prince, surrounded by members of the Organising Committee. His Highness, in a short speech, formally begged the King, in the name of Greece, to take over the stadium, the restoration of which had been rendered possible by the generosity of a great Greek. His majesty, in reply, expressed his admiration for the incomparable beauty of the structure. He also cordially welcomed the athletic youth who had come from all parts of the world to lend brilliance to the festival".

A the end of the brief opening ceremony, Connolly and six others reported for the start of the triple jump; the first event in the modern Olympic Games.

He made his jump - the distance was at 13.71 metres, one metre further that the best by Frenchman Tufferi.
His first jump was enough to give him the immortal distinction of becoming the first Olympic champion of the modern era.
Later in the Games, Connolly won an Olympic silver medal in the high jump and a bronze medal in the long jump.
Two years after his Olympic victory in Athens, Connolly served with the 9th Massachusetts Infantry in the Siege of Santiago in Cuba and later did a spell in the US navy.

In 1912, he ran for the US Congress as a member of the Progressive party. He became a journalist. In 1916, after he had been invited by Colliers Magazine to cover General Pershing's invasion of Mexico. In later years, he became a famous writer, the author of six historical works, nine books of short stories and six novels.

In his autobiography he recalls that he returned to Harvard University. "It was 10 years after Athens before I again set foot in a Harvard building and then it was as guest speaker of the Harvard Union... and the occasion nourished my ego no end".

James Brendan Connolly died in Boston on January 20th, 1957 at the age of 92.

The Princeton Boy

Robert Garrett

Captain Of the American Team

All were stupefied. The Greeks had been defeated at their own classic exercise. They were overwhelmed by the superior skill and daring of the Americans, Robert Garrett, to whom they ascribed a supernatural invincibility enabling them to dispense with training and to win at games which they had never before seen."

Robert Garrett. Princeton student and
Captain of the American team.

Robert S. Garrett (born May 24, 1875 in Baltimore County,) was an American athlete. Robert Garrett was from wealthy family and studied in Princeton University. Robert Garrett excelled in track and field athletics as a student. He was captain of the Princeton track team in both his junior and senior years. Garrett was primarily a shot-putter. Professor William Milligan Sloane, however, suggested he should also try the discus.

They consulted classical authorities to learn about the design of a discus and Garrett hired a blacksmith to make a discus. It weighed nearly thirty pounds and was impossible to throw at any distance, so he gave up on the idea. Garrett paved the way of his three classmates (Francis Lane, third in 100 m, Herbert Jamison, second in 400 m, Albert Tyler second in pole vault) to Athens to compete in the Olympics. When he discovered that a real discus weighs less than five pounds, he decided to enter the event.

The Greek discus throwers were true stylists. Each throw, as they spun, rose from a classical Discobolus stance and was more beautiful than the last. Garrett had no training ; he failed his first two attempts. His final throw, however, sent the discus sailing 19 centimeters beyond the best Greek competitor, Panagiotis Paraskevopoulos's mark.

Garrett also won the shot put and finished second in the long jump and high jump (tied equally with James Connolly).

Later, Garret became a banker and donator to science, especially to history and archeology. He helped to organize and finance an archaeological expedition to Syria, led by Dr. John M. T. Finney. His passion was collecting Medieval and Renaissance Manuscripts. In 1942 Garrett donated to Princeton University his collection of more than 10,000 manuscripts, including sixteen Byzantine Greek manuscripts, containing rare and beautiful examples of illuminated Byzantine Art. He died on April 25th 1951.

Founder of the Olympic Games
Pierre de Coubertin

PIERRE DE COUBERTIN
Founder of the Olympic Games
His heart was buried at Olympia in 1938

Baron Pierre de Coubertin (January 1 1863-September 2, 1937), born as Pierre De Fredy, was a French a educationalist and historian, but is best known as the founder of the modern Olympic Games.

Born in Paris into a noble family, De Coubertin was so inspired by his visits to British and American colleges and universities that he set out to improve education. Part of this improvement would be devoted to sports education, which he believed to be intrinsic to the personal development of young people.

In order to publicise these plans, he organised an International Congress on June 23, 1984 at the Sorbonne in Paris where he proposed to re-instate the ancient Olympic Games. The congress led to the establishment of the International Olympic Committee (IOC) of which de Coubertin became the General Secretary. It was also decided that the first modern Olympics would take place in Athens, Greece. These Games proved a success, and de Coubertin took over the I.O.C. Presidency when Demetrius Vikelas stepped down after the Olympics in his own country.

Despite International Success, the Olympic movement faced hard times, as the 1900 Games (in De Couberin's own Paris) and those of 1904 were both swallowed by international affairs, so receiving little attention.

This changed for the better after the 1906 Summer Olympics, and the Olympic Games went on to become the most important sports event. De Coubertin stepped down from the I.O.C. presidency after the 1924 Olympics in Paris, which proved more successful than the first attempt in the same city in 1900. He was succeeded as president by Belgian, Henri de Bailet-Latour.

De Coubertin remained Honorary President of the IOC until his death in 1937 in Geneva, Switzerland. He was buried in Lausanne (the seat of the I.O.C). although his heart was buried separately in a monument near the ruins of ancient Olympia.

The First Marathon Man
Spiridon Loues

Spiridon Loues
Winner of the Marathon

One summer's day in 490 BC, the Greek legend, Philippides ran 26 hilly miles from Marathon to Athens to deliver the news that the Athenian Army defeated the Persians. Totally exhausted, he died after the good news reached the city.

When the Olympic games were revived in 1894, Michel Breal, a student at the Sorbonne, thought it would be a good idea to have a race commemorating the Pheidippides legend - a twenty six mile race from Marathon to Athens. .On April 10, 1896, the fifth and final day of the Games, twenty-five runners stood at the starting line by the Battle of the Marathon's warrior tomb . A hundred thousand lined Marathon Road. After 2 hours 58 minutes the winner, 23 year old Spiridon Loues, the winner, received a silver medal, a certificate and a laurel-wreath.

Loues became a national hero throughout Greece and was invited to attend the Berlin Games. He gave an olive wreath of peace to Hitler. Loues died in 1940.

Loues wrote in 1936, recalling his victory, " The crowds shouted "Go, Loues, go". That spurred me on. A policeman shouted, "The only ones in front of you are foreigners." "He rode on horseback and had to trot faster to keep up with me".

"A few hundred meters in front of me was an American. I thought "I'll show him" and stepped up the pace. Vasilakos was exhausted and could not keep up. The Frenchman suddenly collapsed. I passed the American and came across an Australian. Everyone shouted "Catch him, Loues, you have got to beat him. Hellas Hellas.." Ambition gripped me. I lengthened my stride. The going was tough. I caught up on him, then an officer shot the pistol into the air and everyone cheered. But he eventually collapsed. I could hear the thunderous roar from the stadium.

All of Greece was there to greet me. I could see my proud father waving to me. The two crown princes joined me in the last lap. I could see the smile of joy on the King's face. I had achieved a great victory for Greece,.

The Olympic Ideal

It is up to you to keep the flag
flying..Olympism is a school
of moral nobility and purity.
De Coubertin.Olympia 1927

What was De Coubertin's original vision? What were the qualities that made up the man'? Why did he set out on this great quest to revive the ancient Games'? The Golden Flame seeks to examine these issues, in the light of the forces working against the new Olympic movement. Has De Coubertin's vision become lost for a new generation'? What was the original philosophy'? Perhaps the Atlanta games will help us focus on the life of De Coubertin, who sacrificed everything in the pursuit of his ideals.

This book attempts to illuminate the life of the man, whose life story and beliefs have become lost among the academic files of sport's history. What is the future of Olympism, as we enter the twenty first century, commercialism has made massive in- roads on the original ideals of the Games. The great and noble vision of De Coubertin's Olympism has suffered under great pressures.

But this was not always the case. Before Montreal and Berlin, there was a time when young men stood beneath the five-ringed flag and the sacred flame, believing in the purer ideals of Olympism. It was a time when nationalism, political gain and profit were monsters that did not erode this great vision. Athens was the re-birth of the ideal.

De Coubertin's story deserves to be told again, if only to inspire the youth of the world today to carry a new torch - to set if alight and to rekindle the 'Golden Flame' - and to discover for themselves that ancient Olympic spirit once more.

***

The American Olympic Team
Princeton and Harvard

The Boston Team

The Olympic ideal is universial .No race or opoch can claim an exclusive monoply on it.
De Coubertin.

The Olympic Gold Medals
and
Diploma

Medal Athens Games 1896
Zeus and Nike

Medal .Athens Games 1896.
Acropolis

OLYMPIC DIPLOMA
DRAWN BY

NIKIFOROS LYTRAS

Citius, Altius, Fortius.

Citius, Altius, Fortius-Faster, Higher, Stronger was the Olympic motto created by Dominican priest and friend of de Coubertin, Pierre Didion (1840-1900). These words were first chiselled in stone over the entrance to Didion's school in 1896 at The Dominican lycee, Albert le Grand, in Paris.

The Olympic rings were adapted and copyrighted by the I.O.C The addition of the colours blue, yellow, black, green and red symbolise the unity of the five continents. De Coubertin presented these coloured rings on a flag at the Paris Congress in 1914. The rings are from the temple of Zeus and carved in stone. De Coubertin discovered them on his visit there in 1896. The statue, built by Lisbon of Elis in 4600, B.C. was regarded as one of the seven wonders of the world.

The Olympic Flame.

The flame is kindled in Olympia under the authority of the I.O.C. The I.O.C. holds all rights relating to the use of the Olympic flame. It was first lit at Olympia in 392 AD. 1544 years later, in 1936, it was re-kindled when the Germans proposed having it brought by torch bearers to Berlin.

THE GOLDEN FLAME

ΔΙΕΘΝΕΙΣ
ΟΛΥΜΠΙΑΚΟΙ
ΑΓΩΝΕΣ
ΑΘΗΝΗΣΙ
1 8 9 6

GABRIEL MURRAY

Ailesbury Publications

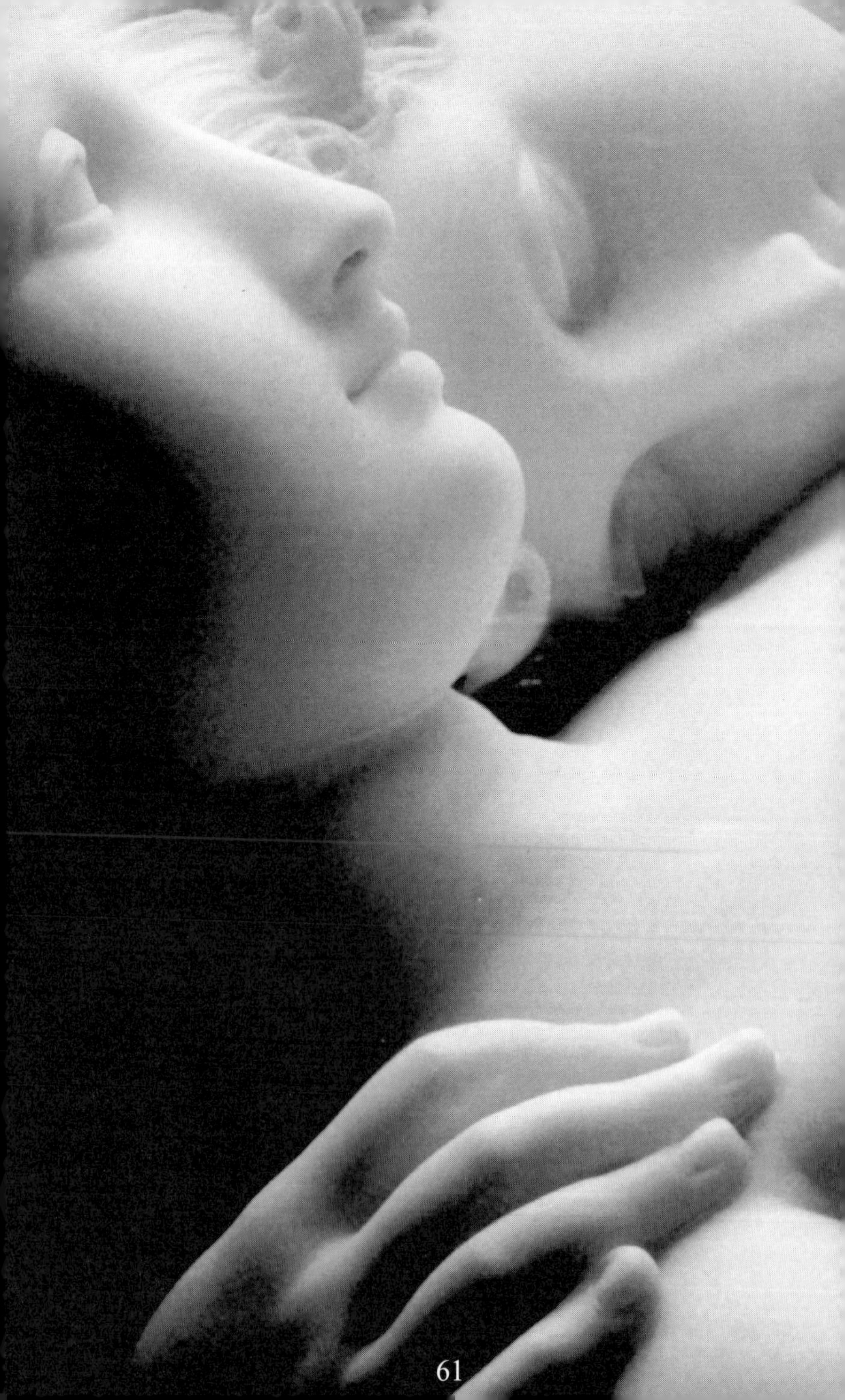

NIKE, GODDESS OF VICTORY.

The Flame on its way to Olympia, 1936

Jessie Owens

There is nothing for Negroes in the Olympics ...The anchient Greeks would turn in their graves if they knew what modern man had made of their holy national games. The next games take place in Berlin in 1936. The blacks must be excluded.

Volkischer Newspaper .Germany 1932

PROLOGUE - LAUSANNE 1936

Olympia, what was the ideal? What was his great dream all about? These questions ran through Pierre de Coubertin's mind as he sat by Lake Geneva. He was an old man now, and his great achievement in Athens, in reviving the ancient Olympics in 1896, had taken place forty years before. The date was the twentieth of July, 1936. Pierre looked at his watch and calculated that at Olympia in Greece the flame would be lit at noon. The sacred flame that would be carried many thousands of miles by torch bearers to Berlin!

The Games were soon to be staged. The Germans had spared no expense in building the stadium and preparing this great showpiece. But Pierre was concerned; it had only been a few weeks since Henri Latour, now President of the International Olympic Committee, had visited him at his house by the shores of the lake. Henri wanted to discuss the speech Pierre had prepared, to be delivered. Was Germany preparing for war? Would the destructive savagery of nationalism ever end?

The German minister for sport, Carl Diem, had requested that Pierre would prepare a recorded message to be broadcast throughout the stadium. It was a speech which Pierre had labored over for many weeks, and he sensed that it would be his last. He tried to distill all his thoughts into one speech, to inform the world of how he saw Olympia and the great ideal. The speech was inconclusive. It had only helped him to focus his thoughts. The Germans, however, had not extended an invitation for him to come to Berlin. Pierre was becoming deeply suspicious of their actions.
He wondered in which wilderness his voice would be crying. It came to him as a sudden, stabbing realization; the thought of being present, but absent from the Games at the same time. It

would be just a trace of him speaking to a vast crowd. Now in old age, he was seeking no further ambition; he just wanted the fight for the ideal. The words he had written about Olympism seemed like small traces in the enormous concourse of time. The Games would be a prelude to a very changed world with premonitions of war to come. His life now seemed like one of the small helpless waves that bob up and down in the sea. It was a cry against the irreversibility of fate. This, he knew, would be his last Olympics.

***

Was it possible that here, by the shores of Lake Geneva, such news should come? Pierre's freckled, yellow hands clutched the arms of a frail wickerwork rocking chair, as he listened to the details of the events of the preceding months. The enduring ideal of a lifetime seemed to be eroded by Henri's report, which came to an unexpected conclusion.

"They have put up a sign", said Henri almost in a whisper.

The chair creaked lazily as Pierre looked up at the formal figure of Henri Latour, who stood with his back to the light. After a while his figure seemed to become spectral, a silhouette in the increasing darkness which had crept into the room. Pierre's brown, coppery eyes opened fully as the monologue came to an end.

He asked the inevitable question with the minimum of movement. It required concentration just to move his dried lips to speak.

"What sign, Henri?"

"Pierre, I can hardly say!"

Henri lost his erect and precise bearing. He seemed to waver in the dying light, as if becoming aware of the consequences his speech may have upon his motionless companion.

"They have put up a sign in the Olympic stadium 'No Jews or dogs'."

Pierre's own feeble hand helped him up from the chair. He kept his eyes closed. Henri watched, motionless, as he stood completely upright. Pierre's creased eyelids were closed, his face silent with the pain of suffering, as one might feel when one is threatened by an overpowering foe. It was not only Pierre's expression of nobility which Henri noticed, but the same stubbornness he had perceived before.

Henri dared not move. The silence had now lapped into the corner of the room. He looked rigid beside the wickerwork chair, from which he had not moved. It seemed as if the shadows were coming up from the basement, as if figures were moving along the walls. It was the evening light coming in from the side windows which made the room seem emptier. Everything had now become bathed in a mellow crimson and lavender light.

It was an atmosphere which the early summer evening always brings; everything had become remote and still. It was a time to think about decisions in perfect solitude. Henri had made up his mind to leave, for if he rested any longer he would suffocate. Pierre spoke to him in slow, measured words; each was infused with the same emphasis.

"Don't you think, Henri...?"

For a brief instant it seemed as if nothing further was to be said. Slowly his eyes began to open; and again Pierre's voice echoed deliberately, emphatically, across the room.

"Henri, don't you think that we should arrange a meeting with Hitler and make him stop this outrage? We have much to do, Henri. I have been thinking over so many things in the last few days, and now I accept that another struggle is ahead of us. We believed in progress once, Henri; nothing seemed more natural to us."

Then Pierre continued, "We know that the world thought that it was no longer possible to believe in such an ideal, but we continue to believe in it. That is why you must go to Berlin and speak the simple words of Olympism. The ideal must be observed, and no host country will destroy it. It is too late to call off the games, but in this case we must make a protest to Germany, should these displays of anti-Semitism continue. It must be done, Henri. We both know what a reputation people have for twisting the truth such people have. Take care of the flame, Henri, take care of the flame!"

Henri could hardly speak; all the feelings of loyalty and respect which he had entertained for Pierre over thirty years seemed to flood back, releasing the stiffness of formal courtesy. He realized now the depth of the emotional bonds which underlay their conversation and work over the years. This was the most mysterious bond of all, the bond of love, which two people have through facing things together. The figure of Pierre seemed to shrink again, by the light coming from the window that covered his delicate outline. Henri held back the tears of unspoken love. Pierre had claimed his total loyalty and unqualified admiration. He knew that he was indeed coming to the end of his life. Yet he had to face this last enormous struggle.
It was a shock to see Pierre resume his old vigor and prepare to challenge the German government. Apart from the way he said, "Henri", the voice was almost unrecognizable. It was as if he was no longer used to speaking. It was the voice of a man who had been abandoned by the fates.

The way he pronounced Henri's name was an echo of earlier years. As the sounds of Pierre's voice trailed away, the conversation came to an end. The hour was getting late; they were now standing in the twilight.

Henri made to bow and leave, stumbling over the few words. "I will return to see you soon; meanwhile, my thanks for receiving me so kindly." A tiny movement of Pierre's neat, frail hand acknowledged this courtesy. Henri took his leave from the room with a short bow. If he had stayed any longer he would have had an attack of vertigo.

***

Pierre examined his files again, filled with letters, news clippings and notes on the Berlin Games. Something about the Games had gone amiss - the great ideals of Olympism were now under attack.

Hitler stated in his speech on May 21st, 1935:

"The principal effect of every war is to destroy the power of the nation. Germany needs peace and desires peace! Whoever lights the torch of war in Europe can wish for nothing but chaos. We, however, live in the firm conviction that in our time will be fulfilled not the decline but the renaissance of the west."

Since 1933 the Jews had been subject to a rein of terror. Because of an international outcry this terror had been limited. Under the Nuremburg Laws the segregaton of races increased. On June 2nd, 1933 Jews were excluded from sports organizations. Julius Stricher wrote in the newspaper Sturmer:

"Jews are Jews and they have no place in German sport. Germany is the fatherland of Germans, not Jews, and the Germans have the right to do what they want in their own country."

In 1932 the National Socialists had used similar language while referring to black athletes. Another newspaper, the Volkischer Beobachter, stated:

"There is nothing for Negroes at the Olympics... The ancient Greeks would turn in their graves if they knew what modern man had made of their holy national games... The next games take place in Berlin in 1936... The blacks must be excluded."

Pierre read the report from the June 6th meeting in 1933 of the International Olympic Committee in Vienna, which outlined the United States' proposal to boycott the Olympic Games, because of the Jewish issue. On November 21st of that year the American Amateur Athletic Union voted to boycott the games.

This resolution was supported by most members, including Avery Brundage, President of the Olympic Committee. In June 1934, Brundage went to Germany to discover for himself what the situation was. The Nazis knew of his arrival and he found little evidence of abuse of the Jews. On his return he recommended that America take part in the games. But new evidence continued to emerge of terrorism against the Jews.
Pierre leafed through his papers once again and found a letter with the stamp of the American I.O.C. It was from General Charles Sherill, who met with Hitler on 24th August 1935.
There the General had requested a firm commitment from Hitler that Jews would be allowed to compete on German teams. Three months later, on December 8th, it was decided by a margin of two and one half votes to send America to the Olympics. The die was cast.

Pierre sat back in his chair and opened another file. In it were some photos of Leni Riefenstahl and an article on her film, 'Olympia.' It was a giant epic approved by Dr. Goebbels, Minister for Propaganda. She planned on filming the flame being taken from Olympia to Berlin. But was it a film about the Olympic spirit, Pierre wondered, or just another German propaganda film? Soon the Games would be staged. The first draft of his speech had been sent to Berlin months ago. He had no time now to change and modify it. Pangs of anxiety flashed through his mind - was it too late to stop the Berlin Olympics?

The visit of Henri was as he had feared. The former guarantee which the Germans had given had no value. It was broken at the first opportunity. Their concession to a moral principle meant nothing, other than stalling. It was an excuse used time and time again by these people. They made pretence of agreement and waited to have the first opportunity to breach the code. Their cynicism even allowed them the pretence of good behavior.

On Pierre's desk were spread small oval photographs and pens in malachite stands. He looked for the brown bundle with the blue silk ribbon, which held the details of a meeting in Vienna in 1933, three years before.

Henri Baillet-Latour, his successor, was now responsible for all the organizational details of the Games. The Germans had been awarded the Games with a postal vote of forty three to sixteen, with eight abstentions.
There were already suspicions of what was to come. There was a clear undertaking, confirmed by Henri's request. The official representatives of the German Reich would guarantee the observance in full of the Olympic Charter. In principle, the German Jews would not be excluded from the Games of the Eleventh Olympiad.

Pierre could see even then that the representatives of the Reich were powerless. Their leader had been Chancellor of Germany for only six months. He wanted the Games to be a showpiece to the world. The thirty first sessions in Vienna had hardly closed when Hitler made his first move. He always bluffed to see how far he could go. That was the method of his foreign policy. Both presidents of the organizing committees, one for the Berlin Games, the other for the 9th Garmisch Winter Games, were to be replaced. Then Henri had acted decisively. The suspension of the presidents of the German games on anti-Semitic grounds had been challenged. If Pierre's two colleagues, Dr. Lewald and Ritter von Halt, should cease to be presidents of the Organizing Committees, the IOC would be obliged to withdraw the Games from Garmisch and Berlin.

The Germans had appointed a minister with responsibility for sport, to bring the political aspects of the games into line with other areas of national life. They had stated that 'Germany's destiny would be great'. The simple truths, however, had been distorted by Hitler. Germany was now one nation, politically unified by a single absolute ruler. The Olympic Games were of fundamental importance to the Germans' aims. They would show to the world the most modern of Olympic stadiums, based on classical models. Germany was renewing its pride and would demonstrate the 'triumph of its will'.

Pierre had stood up to the unwarranted intrusion. He sought redress for the explicit anti-Semitism which lay behind this interference. Under pressure the two men were re-instated. It seemed that a moral victory had been won; it was an acknowledgement of the power of the Olympic ideal. Hitler had given way before this threat.

It was understandable that Pierre and Henri did not want to face a second interview. The promise made in 1933 had been broken. The power of Hitler had grown and the full depth of anti-Semitism was now apparent. Under the Nuremberg Laws the Nazis defined the Jews as sub-human. Now that the Games were so close, perhaps Hitler felt that he could break the previous agreements. It could be argued that the real issue behind the dismissal of Lewald and von Halt had not been dealt with. Pierre re-read the notes. It was in consideration of the stature of Dr. Lewald and von Halt that the IOC granted the organization of the Games to Berlin and Garmisch. Everyone was aware of the reasons for their removal, and the protest by the I.O.C. made direct reference to their Jewish origins.

Henri Baillet-Latour had come to Pierre that evening with neither the composure of a man of authority, nor the self-assurance of a man of his class. For over twenty years he had dealt with the problems of international organization. Henri was the quintessential committee man. He was nevertheless frequently mistaken for a retiring introvert. However, he was always familiar, even to a stranger. It appeared as if one had always known him.

Henri had approached the meeting with Hitler in a mood of deepening apprehension. He knew that there was more to him than ordinary rumors had suggested. He appealed to all the old prejudices of Germany. Hitler felt that German destiny had been thwarted by the oppressive treaty of Versailles. He had a consuming need for power, which he called "My struggle". Beneath his facade was his absolute search for superiority.

Pierre slowly placed the papers back in the bundle. Each one had a small pencil number on the top right hand corner. His period of retirement had been spent in putting a lifetime of notes and papers in order. Now he was acting as archivist to his own past. Some days he could only go through a few papers. The emotion of seeing once again letters from those long since dead, made the work slow and difficult. Sometimes a note would bring back a whole rush of memory, which had been obliterated. It survived now, almost physically, in the small pieces of paper in front of him. At times the faded gilt-edged menus identified every kind of sensation and memory. For a moment it seemed he could taste and hear the past. Henri would return again soon. He would wait to hear of the news of this meeting with Hitler with a deep sense of anxiety.

***

OLYMPIA-BERLIN. 1936

The route of the flame wound its way along the Greek coast from Olympia, to Krestena, Zacharo, Kuparizza, Philiatre, Chora, Kallamat, Sparta, Tripolis, Napoleon and Corinth, from there to Meara and on to Eludis, then finally to Athens. Everywhere it came it was received, welcomed and greeted. The flame of Olympia was on its way to the north of Europe. It was Pierre's hope that the power of the symbol would overcome the forces of darkness.

Over three thousand runners were assembled along the route, all exposed to the elements of the sun, wind and rain. The torches, made of German steel, were over two feet long. Their magnesium heads could burn in the wind and rain. They were followed by numerous cars, among them Sandy Duncan from the British Olympic Association, who traveled behind in a Rolls Royce. His sole mission was to protect the flame.

Across the plains of Greece the flame was carried. By day and night it traveled, northwards into Bulgaria and Yugoslavia, and followed the railway line of the Orient Express. At every border the flame was handed over to the runners of the next country in a formal ceremony. In Hungary the flame was greeted as a great moment for all nations.

At night, hundreds gathered on the mountain ridges to observe it approaching across the vast Hungarian plain. The gypsies played music to the passing torch and in Budapest, where it was greeted by thousands of people, the king of the gypsies performed at a special ceremony.

Between Budapest and the Austrian border the runners made a special detour so that the flame could pass through the mining villages, where the runners were given an Olympic greeting.

The torch carried the spirit of ancient Olympia, and it animated those who observed it crossing the vast plains of southern Europe, inspiring heroic hopes for the future. Pierre could feel it coming closer, and he knew that some hundreds of miles to the east the flame would be passing through Austria. There were cries of "Eleen!" as the torch made its way through the last Hungarian villages; echoes of the same cry made in Athens forty years before. On the Austrian border the flame was handed to Doctor Schmidt, the president of the Olympic association. A wave of excitement washed across Austria as the torch reached Vienna. It unleashed intense emotions in the vast crows that had gathered there outside the Hofburg Palace.

Searchlights picked out the runner against a black sky, and when he eventually reached the gates of the Palace, the chant of "Hitler. Hitler," could be heard. There the runner paused to light the sacred flame of the gates. The intensity of expectation seemed to increase as the flame approached Germany on July 31st. Fifty thousand people were waiting on both sides of the Czech-German border in the village of |Hellendorf when the exchange of the torch was made, extraordinary applause broke out with the words, "We salute the youth of the world."

The news that the 'Golden Flame' had reached Germany created a feeling of emotion across the land. Hundreds of people gathered at the village squares, and bands and trumpet players announced its arrival. All through Saxony the route was lined by people, cheering on the flame through Dresden and Meissen.

BERLIN 1936

On the morning of August 1st, just after eleven thirty, the flame reached the southern corner of Berlin, where the Brandenburg Gate was covered in green garlands and swastika flags. The flame had reached the Olympic city, where an extra million visitors were present to greet its arrival.

The members of the International Olympic Committee, along with Henri Latour, assembled at the old museum. There, Goering and Goebbels received them and led them up the front steps. The trumpet sounded, and the flags were raised. The large neo-classical facade loomed up before them. Then Goebbels's voice boomed across the vast audience. "Holy flame burn, burn and never go out!'
A strange silence fell across the crowd. Then a faint murmur arose slowly, followed by a trickling sound that came in an unnerving patter. It was the noise of cheering, of thousands of voices shouting the words, "The flame! The flame!" Then, like a great wind, the cheers came rapidly, rising to a crescendo like a great symphony, spreading like fire into the crowds, to the Lustgarden, emerging as an intense roar.

It had been twelve days and eleven nights since the sacred flame had left Olympia. The single runner was followed by hundreds of supporters running behind him. Thousands of hands rose up in a Nazi salute as the torch approached the guests of honor. Over a half a million people watched the flame as it reached the stadium. Then the sound of the crowd cheering could be heard. It echoed through the stadium like wind across a field of corn waves sweeping across a windswept sea. Everyone was filled with a great feeling of emotion.

A large, open, black Mercedes Benz swept out of the Chancellery and sped along Wilhelmstrasse. Hitler, in army uniform, rode standing in the front of his car, with his left hand resting on the windscreen and the right hand saluting to the crowd. The cavalcade swept through the Brandenburg Gate. Great cheers rose from the crowd. Behind was the torch bearer traveling the same route dressed in white, followed by twenty four runners in white and black, in a v-shaped position, all running in step. Hitler's car halted at the Bell Tower where he was greeted by the sight of fifty two national teams. Trumpets sounded from the towers of the Marathon Gate.

Henri Latour greeted Hitler and walked with him across the grounds of the stadium. A great cry emerged from the crowd. Henri told Pierre of that moment of apprehension, the final moment when the Olympic ideal went into battle against another but darker symbol. It was a moment of deep anxiety for Henri, because the symbol was now handed over for the period of the Games. Crossing the arena, the Fuhrer received a bouquet of flowers from the daughter of the organizer of the Games, Karl Diem. Then the sounds of Wagner's 'March of Homage' were heard. A wave of emotion rose up again among the crowd. Then flags were hoisted all around the rim of the stadium. The huge Olympic bell began to toll.

The teams began to march past, led by the Greeks. Then he appeared: Pierre's old friend Spiridon Loues, leading the field, was clad in traditional Greek dress. He had won the Marathon in Athens in 1896; he was now sixty years old. Loues approached Hitler and handed him a wild olive branch from the sacred grove of Olympia. Loues said, "I present to you this olive branch as a symbol of love and peace. We hope that the nations will ever meet solely in such peaceful competition". Pierre told Henri of his surprise that Loues had turned up in Berlin. It seemed that Loues had spanned the Games of two eras, like an ancient Greek hero who had come back to life.

When the French team appeared, there was a huge roar from the crowd, as if the Germans were prepared to bury the past and seek a new peace with the French. Was the threat of war now less likely, in these moments? Had the Olympics the ability to dissolve hatred, as in ancient Greece?

After the march past, Dr. Lewald spoke to the vast crowd:

"In a few moments the torch bearer will appear to light the Olympic fire on his tripod, and then it will rise, flaming to heaven, for the weeks of this festival. It creates a real and spiritual bond of fire between our German fatherland and the sacred places of Greece founded 4,000 years ago by our Nordic immigrants..."

Then Pierre's speech could be heard crackling over the loudspeakers. Henri assured him that it came across loud and clear, and that it was solemnly listened to by the vast audience. Henri, however, couldn't help wondering whether this message of comradeship and the Olympic spirit had been accepted by the Germans.

The Fuhrer stepped forward and declared the Games of the Modern Era open. The huge, five-ringed Olympic flag was raised and guns boomed in salute; twenty thousand pigeons were released and flew out of the stadium into the sky, each carrying a colored ribbon. Then Richard Strauss, the composer, stood on the Olympic rostrum and conducted the Olympic hymn, Schiller's Ode to Joy, in the choral setting of the conclusion to Beethoven's Ninth Symphony.

A massed choir opened the Olympiad with this intense demonstration of Beethoven's love of democracy and the free spirit that belonged to what was best in German culture.

The music rose above the audience and the assembled statesmen and crowned heads of Europe. It seemed that the music soared above all the bitter nationalism of the time, bringing back again the true internationality of humanity, where peace and the arts could flourish, expressed in Schiller's words to joy. "Ye Millions, 0 Ye Millions I embrace you."

All eyes turned to the eastern Gate as it came to the end. Then it appeared, the flame: 'The Golden Flame,' carried by the final torch bearer, the blond Berliner named Schilgen. A tremendous cry arose from the crowd as he ran towards the steps, to the tripod that held the fire bowl. It was as if some mythical runner from Ancient Greece had traversed endless time, emerging into the modern era. It was a memorable moment for Henri who looked on with bated breath, along with the vast audience.

Schilgen climbed the steps, then paused at the top and lifted his torch high. For a moment it seemed as if history was frozen. This could have been Olympia two thousand years before. Silence gripped the crowd, whilst he placed the blazing torch to the bowl; then the flame burned gloriously.

***

LAUSANNE - 1937

Henri related to him how Loues approached the Fuhrer and handed him an olive branch, plucked from the sacred grove of Olympia. The old victor, Loues, had shaken the hand of a man who did not respect the Olympic ideal. In his innocence, he was not aware of what this hand was capable of.

Henri and Pierre spoke of this moment as the evening sun began to set over the lake. They spoke of Loues and what he symbolized and of how he had been persuaded by the Nazis to come to Berlin. Pierre could see him again and share with him the memories of Athens. Loues focused his mind on his thoughts and what it was once all about. Pierre looked across the waters and thought back to Athens. On that great day, all his work and all his dreams had borne fruit, at the opening of the first Olympic Games. Pierre looked across the waters and thought back to Athens. On that great day, all his work and all his dreams had borne fruit, at the opening of the first Olympic Games.

But the Berlin games now seemed far away; the days had passed rapidly since Henri had first visited him. It was as if he had lived in limbo. Living by Lake Geneva and taking walks had done little to enliven his spirit. The last few months had awoken him from his numbness, and the events in Berlin caused him to think again. What was the ideal of the Games? What had it been, what had it become?

Looking through the speeches over the years, he realized that he had failed to speak out clearly about the ideals of Olympism. Some of the language was vague and poetic. He had spoken of "A drunkenness of the blood, the ruthlessness of sport" and "the democracy of internationalism; the paradox of patriotism and "the banner of Olympia in the concourse of nations".

He looked back on the years since Athens that had been absorbed in details, arrangements, meetings, organization; the constant callers and domestic tragedy. It was painful to think of it, his own son Jacques left out in the sun; its rays giving him a stroke, robbing him of his mental powers. His daughter Renee, from an early age, had shown signs of melancholy and unhappiness. The critical moments of his life had passed. There was a sense of failure. The fates had pursued him and his children. Like so much of ancient tragedy, the sacrifices of the fathers were visited upon their offspring.

***

Here in exile, he seemed to live in three worlds: the world he now knew, confined to a few small rooms and listening to the lake; the world he remembered, far from here; Paris and Normandy, and the world he had always imagined; Olympia.

By the shores of Lake Geneva he felt at home. It was a place of contemplation. But the mystery of its waters, with its passive resignation, had been deceptive. He had contemplated its moods and its changes. It had brought him to a state of meditation, and the restlessness of his search was calmed. The floating images raced through the night and somehow could be powerfully recalled at any time, so deeply were they embedded. He began to remember experiences of his past, images that spoke of a particular place, the loveliest in all Hellas, Olympia.

It came back to him now: the memories, the flame, the ideal. He was filled for a moment with a deep sense of nervous exhaustion. What was to become of his ideal? He had learned from Henri that the Germans had not acted honorably in observing the Olympic charter; racism, nationalism and propaganda had entered the events of the Berlin Games.

His present world was small and familiar. He had a sense of home by the shores of Lake Geneva. He felt liberated when out on the lake rowing his boat. There, out on its glassy waters, he was well away from callers and the slow encroaching burdens of his life. A sense of home now did not depend on the familiar domestic surroundings. He found home out on these lapping waters which had the colour of liquid silver, changing to deepest greenish blue. Watching the even ripples of the water, he felt calm and serene. He listened to the water with its constant rippling movements. It was the easiest thing in the world to sink down and release oneself into the mystery of its depths.

The days here in Lausanne seemed to follow a fixed order. Marie had gone on one of her journeys, which over the years had become more and more frequent and lasted a greater length of time. For Marie, a recent flu justified another long trip to her favorite doctor. There she recovered slowly among the mountain peaks. During these absences Pierre was left alone in the house.

He sat beside the lake late into the afternoon. The sun had just begun to set. The course of the sun could be followed from the light on the lake. It began as a powerful illumination. Then it turned to a sheet as smooth and transparent as glass. Towards evening, one could see the shadows in its cooling depths.

At midday the sun was high. A kind of ashen haze rose in the air. The hulls of the boats were as spiders' webs glinting in the sun. By the trees, one could see the light rippling upwards and downwards in movements as rapid as the blink of an eye. For Pierre the trees by the lake were a consoling presence. Like great lungs they breathed life, spreading their scent in the cool evening breeze

***

Henri's last visit had left Pierre in a state of suspended animation. For days he had wandered around the house. In the evening he would go down to the lake, to where the water absorbed the golden rays reflected by the declining sun. Boats glided through the placid surface making long lines of white foam. The crying gulls followed. Their grey-tipped wings touched the surface as they descended suddenly.

Pierre could drift into a mood of oblivion and forgetfulness by this lake. The anxiety of Henri's visit and the menace which was hanging over the Games could be forgotten.

Pierre lived here like an orphan. He received the charity of the city, with the gift of a house. He had been reduced almost to a state of childish dependence. He had spent all his money on the Games, now he had to pay the price.

In preparation for Henri's next visit he began to look over papers from the last fifty years. He read again copies of speeches made long ago. He had kept these carefully locked away. He realized that these were an important account of his life. In some precise way these speeches could be pieced together.

He spent less time now walking down by the shore. His rowing had been severely reduced. More and more of his time had been spent in his study. At first he had leafed slowly through his papers, but each one gave him a small jolt of excitement.

At night he looked out over the lake and across to the slopes. A small crescent moon had begun to pass over one side. Its shape was just a small opening in the deep, inky- blue darkness of the sky. The houses and villas shone in the darkness. It seemed as if some of them were suspended in the sky, having no contact with the earth. Along the side of one slope ran little beads of illuminations. A large red and yellow source of light caught the eye. The water was dark, as if everything was consumed by its black -ness.

He sat out on the balcony. It was unusually warm for the time of evening. The thought of retiring early was a mockery in such balmy weather. He often sat out there, wrapped in a blanket under the stars. They always looked closer and brighter as the moon began to wax in its new cycle. Nothing was more beautiful than to watch the moon grow full. On certain evenings it disappeared behind the peaks to the east. He watched its yellow brown colours which hung on the passing clouds. The slate roof tops became silvery blue. The floating diamond mesh across the lake was full of ripples of light.

The moonlight reminded him of the picture by Caspar David Friedrich. The frock-coated man in the painting bore a resemblance to the philosopher, Nietzsche, looking out from a promontory, all the time observing the moon across the sea. All around was the loneliness of the lake whispering a deep, sad, music. Its melancholy sounds moved restlessly in his soul.

He began to concentrate on his past. He tried to focus his mind on his past dreams. His destiny had become bound up with a search for an ideal. His life had been mapped out by certain events of his youth. He tried to remember all those emotions, now stored away in his memory. He tried to recall what the reasons for his quest were. He wondered what events in his life had changed him and which ones had fulfilled him. But he knew instinctively that the most important moments of his life were connected to Olympia and the Athens Games of 1896. Now he could sit quietly beside the lake and remember.

***

The Flame on the Greek Border travelling North to Berlin

Belgian, Henri Latour, president of the of the
International Olympic Committe
A loyal friend of De Coubertin in his final days

CHAPTER ONE

PARIS 1870

To all comes
The wave of death and falls unforeseen
Even on him who foresees it.
But honour grows for the dead
Whose tender repute a God fosters.
One came, a Champion,
To the great navel of broad-bosomed earth,
In the floor of Pytho he lies

Neoptolemos
He sacked Troy's city.
NEMEAN

VII Louis XIV Pierre's family were enobled by PARIS. 1870.

For Pierre the struggle to remember the time of life during which one grows up was not difficult. His recollection of this early period seemed clear. It was the time of his most intense experience. All that had happened seemed immediate and momentous. Everything he could think of now was so deeply colored in retrospect. He wondered if the impressions which were so intense then had not been a mirage. But it was the shackling of his freedom which distinguished this time.

What could he recall of the College St Ignace situated by the Rue Madrid? His Jesuit education was at the newly founded day school. His parents had sent him there, entrusting him to the care of priests, who would attempt to control their difficult and rebellious son.

All this time from his childhood the scene was condensed into one image: the image of a burning city. As a boy he had spent many hours in his father's library where he would read, in the leather-bound volumes of ancient books, of lost kingdoms, magical cities and great heroes.

It was, however, one dream, a sequence of images, which revived his memory of his father's library with its special colored rows of books in blue, green and bright red. It was a large room with a painted ceiling and carved mahogany bookcases lining the walls. Over the doorway there were shelves for what his mother called baby books, all of them in olive green covers. They were little prayer books and small books for children. From one of them he was shown the picture of Aeneas carrying his father, Anchises, from the ruins of Troy in flames.

This book was Homer's Iliad. It recorded the events of the Trojan wars; how the Trojans had been tricked by Odysseus the Greek, and how men had entered beyond the walls of the great city of Troy in the belly of a wooden horse. It was the Laocoon, the Trojan priest, who had warned the Trojans of the Greek deception. But this Trojan hero would meet death, strangled by a giant snake.

Pierre had been told a little about this hero by his father, as it was linked to his family memory: in the fourteenth century the Laocoon's statue had been discovered by one of his relatives in the grounds of a villa near Rome.

He remembered observing the illustration of the giant towers of Troy burning, symbolizing one of the great battles of the western world. But all of this seemed fused in his memory with the burning city of Paris. He was only seven years old when the Prussians began their bombardment of the city. He had been sitting in the library, quietly reading one of the large volumes. He remembered listening to his sister tinkling on the piano in the drawing-room, and the wind whispering through the curtains of the French windows, which opened onto the gardens.

He remembered the shattering noise - the crash of splintered glass, of flames racing through the house, of books on fire, and within a moment 'the great towers' were burning once again. The flames licked and struggled their way up the bookshelves, reaching towards the ceiling. In a moment all of Pierre's vision was filled with these flames. Troy and Paris were burning. From his childhood until now this image remained in his memory. For many months, at night, he had this restless dream of a library burning.

His mother had heard him scream and came to his room. She displayed that tenderness which she always showed towards him. She alone understood the source of his upset. Each night it returned. When his mother brought the book for him to see where the picture first appeared it did nothing to lessen his discomfort.

Pierre observed the figure coming down from a parapet, of Aeneas. He wore a long helmet that looked like two scalloped rabbit ears. He carried an old bearded man, with a hooped cowl. At his side was a little boy, staring ahead. In the background a turret was consumed by flames. Small figures with spears and shields ran for their lives. But in Pierre's dream the little boy was burning. So too was the library.

The flames crackled and climbed throughout the houses, shooting upwards, across the streets of the city, licking and pushing their way up along the walls. Paris was burning, and the city was engulfed in dark smoke and the smell of charred wood. The Seine was filled with dancing reflections, and along the street people ran for safety, some jumping into its waters, drowning in its swift icy flow.

On the first floor, Pierre stood at his bedroom window dressed in a blue sailor suit. He was disturbed by what he was now observing, but unaware of its implications. These were the flames caused by the Prussian bombardment of Paris and the last onslaught of the Franco-Prussian War. The Germans had moved steadily across France and reached the city walls. At first they had taken Alsace Lorraine, the disputed German territory, and then moved westwards, like a plague cutting through the French resistance. Now the city was about to fall. Pierre watched in awe as the dancing crackling flames moves towards the house. For the young Pierre, this was fantasy come to life. He remembered looking at the large etchings that illustrated Virgil's Aeneid and spoke of the last days of the city of Troy. It too was burned to the ground by the Greeks. The wise Ulysses had crossed the Aegean to Troy followed by hundreds of Greek warships to reclaim the most beautiful woman of the ancient world.

Pierre had sat at his mother's reading desk in the library and peered at the plates of Troy. He observed images of burning towers, like the great symbols of the Tarot cards. Men, women and children jumped for their lives from these ancient towers to certain death. A little boy of seven could not understand the terror behind this destructive war. It was something that belonged to the past. Now another war had become a reality. Paris was now at the mercy of this bombardment continued.

It had only been days before that his mother had told him that this ancient city had once belonged to myth, and had been discovered by a German named Schliemann who had ventured to the shores of Turkey, many years before. With his considerable wealth he began excavations for this lost mythical city. He, too, had looked on these illustrations to the Aeneid and dreamt of finding this city that gave birth to the greatest classic of the ancient world penned by the old bard Homer.

***

Pierre was interrupted by the maid, Babette, who scolded him for standing near the window and made him undress and put on his long white laced night shirt. But her efforts to put Pierre to sleep were to no avail. Her attempts at a kind of normality were pointless as he, too, could observe her nervousness. Where was. Mama and Papa, he asked, Babette replied that they would come and say goodnight later. But a pattern had been broken. He longed for this nightly tucking in, the sweet smile of his mother illuminated by lamplight. He remembered her sweet kiss and most of all the delicate fragrance of her perfume she always wore. No, it was not to be; the continuity that he always had been used to was broken. It was a tiny echo of the daily occurrences outside the window. This little child of seven and his world had been turned upside down forever.

Babette left him with closed eyes which soon opened to observe the burning city. The flames danced across the walls, their shadows projected in wonderful patterns.

He sat up and looked towards the silhouette of flames and waited for his Mama to come but soon fell asleep and into a tormented dream. Inseparable in his mind, scenes of Paris burning mingled with those of Troy. Disturbed by the images that filed his mind with a searing white light, Pierre tossed and turned in his bed. A face appeared covered in blood; the face of a Greek soldier, with a spear driven deep into his chest falling from a burning tower and through endless space. Pierre was falling too. Nothing could stop his passage through an endless void.

***

Pierre de Coubertin 1863 - 1937
MarieRohan de Coubertin 1859 - 1963

CHAPTER TWO

PARIS 1888

Charioteer most High
Of the unweary-footed lightning,
Zeus, thy circling Hours have sent me
With the gamut of the harp's song
To witness the loftiest of Games
When friends fare well.

OLYMPIAN IV

Louis xiv depicted as an Olympian, carrying the flame

PARIS 1884

Pierre awoke from his dream and wiped the sweat from his brow. He looked about the room, but he could see no flames dancing upon the walls. Only a painting, in shadowed light from an oil lamp, illuminated the image of the Prussian onslaught of Paris. His childhood memory flickered through his mind. Now he was no longer a boy but a young cadet of nineteen at the St Cyr Military Academy, not far from Paris.

But why walk in the footsteps of these men that had engaged in pointless wars? Why had he begun on this path? Yes, it was his father's wish that he attend St Cyr, one of France's finest academies. But he had been there for six months now and had become increasingly dissatisfied. Every morning the cadets were woken by a bugle call. Pierre would fall out of bed before sunrise, put on his well-polished boots and immaculately pressed uniform and walk down the long tiled corridor to the court-yard for inspection. Pierre, however, was not one for believing in the authority of his superiors. Each young man had been trained to take the reins of control with an authoritarian firmness and calculated decisiveness which would send his troops to death or victory. General Derome addressed them.

"Gentlemen, the war with the Prussians began in 1870.

Nothing could stop them. They cut across France like a scythe through a field of ripe corn. Who is not aware of this date of the indescribable scene of carnage when the Prussians slaughtered our men despite their valiant resistance? You must be ready to place your lives under our command-ready to fight to the death for France.
General Derome stood and reviewed the glittering line of young cadets, crisp in their crimson uniforms. They were struck by his

penetrating stare, which was directed towards them.

Before leaving them to return to their dormitories and prepare for dinner, General Derome turned to speak again.

"In defeat, we will find strength. Never again will France suffer this humiliation."

"You, gentlemen, are the chosen few; we must never make a mistake again. Alsace is bartered territory-you know that war could come any day. We must always be prepared. Tomorrow, so that none of you may forget, you will be taken to the site of our most bitter loss. Tomorrow you must learn how to turn defeat into victory. Vive la France! You are dismissed."

In retrospect Pierre looked at this time as one of painful monotony, a low, unpleasant pain like the nausea one associates with being on a boat on the swelling sea. The deepest discomfort was not to know how long this painful experience would continue.

The General had implanted in their minds that on them depended the protection of honor, the restoration of the country and the defense of France. The defeat at Loingly was burnt into their memories, with the distinct image of a landscape covered in crosses. But one could erase in the glassy mirror of the mind those exact memories, recollections like the bedroom of one's childhood, or the smell of freshly cut grass. The eye had taken note of those crimson colored fields. Now, by the strangest alchemy, the image emerged of a whole landscape covered in thousands of white crosses. Pierre remembered standing on the ridge himself, overlooking that plain of crimson and white.

This image seemed to be layered among the other images of his youth: the memories of burning, of the siege of Paris, and the defeat of Troy. Again, the memory of the war of the Greeks came to him in those restless nights of sleep at St Cyr. He remembered the images of Troy. History had been repeated and another city, Paris, named after a Trojan hero, had suffered the same fate, burning like Troy.

The Iliad had taught him the futility of war; it consigned lives to Hades, to darkness. From war there are no victors. War reduces all to the same condition. No one recovers from its destruction. Achilles had grieved when he killed his friend Hector; it was a lamentation that echoed throughout all wars. The victor was presented as a hero, but the more deeply wounded victim, the one he had loved, was dead. Outwardly he was the victor, but inwardly he had lost. Pierre refused to conform to an education that would teach him how to lead men to their deaths. By a single thrust of circumstance, he would learn to look for peace.

Within the struggle to understand himself he grew silent, as one does. The figure of the Trojan priest who, with all his strength, opposed the forces of the sea which were sent to punish him came to mind. This was the decision of Athena. "I fear the Greeks even when they bear gifts" said the Laocoon. But Athena gave her judgment, and serpents were sent from the sea to strangle him and his sons.

Pierre had decided that he would leave the Academy no matter how long it took. Such a life had no meaning for him. He would not abandon what he understood that evening, as the white crosses turned to red in the setting sun. He would not abandon that single absolute intuition; he would not submit, be it to his father's domination or to the rituals of the army. They had taught him nothing.

Now he would search for a single idea that was not absorbed in the world of power, greed, vengeance or hatred. He would struggle with this uncertain fate.

Pierre remembered how at this time he began to receive letters from Paris. They were from Marie, whom he had met by the sea at Balbec some months before.
Marie's letters consoled him in the hours of distress and loneliness. She would enclose poems and news of Paris. The poem by Byrom came to mind, echoed by his feelings for her.

Yes - it was Love - if thoughts of tenderness,
Tried in temptation, strengthened by distress,
Unmoved by absence, firm in every clime,
And yet - Oh more than all! - untired by time;
Which nor defeated hope, not baffled wile,
Could render sullen were she ne'er to smile,
Nor rage could fire, nor sickness fret to vent
On her one murmur of his discontent,
Which still would meet with joy, with calmness part,
Lest that his look of grief should reach her heart;
Which nought removed, nor menaced to remove;
If there be love in mortals - this was love!

***

Francis Fredy was captain of the kings ships.
Henri Louis de Coubertin was guilliotined by
the revolutionaries.
The Bourbon king awarded the title
of Baron to the De Coubertin family in 1821

CHAPTER THREE

VERSAILLES 1890

Mother of the gold-crowned Games,
Olympia, mistress of truth,
Where seers interpret burnt offerings
And test the bright thunderer Zeus
If he has any word about men
Who yearn in their hearts to win great glory.

OLYMPIAN VIII

Palace of Versailles, The Gallery of Glass

VERSAILLES 1890

Permission to attend a ball in Parisian society was not difficult to obtain. After several months at St. Cyr Military Academy one was allowed a weekend away. Pierre had delayed accepting such a privilege until he knew that a decent interval had elapsed. Only one matter had remained in his mind: Marie, who was now in attendance at one of the salons in Paris.

She was the daughter of Monsieur De Rothan. Marie had sometimes visited Pierre's residence at number two, Rue de Odinot. This was the girl with whom Pierre went for walks through parks and arcades extending as far as the eye could see. From the day they met, they knew that their future together would be a romantic one. It had become an adventure that the young Marie could never have thought possible. Everywhere in Paris there were buildings designed by the Baron de Hausmann. Those who had lived right in the centre of the city were slowly moved to the outskirts. For Marie and Pierre, the naming of the new buildings was a favorite occupation. It was said that he intended to make this city fit for a Roman legion. Paris was to be made into a new Athens. It would echo the past in all its glory.

Marie's looks were considered to be Russian. Her eyes were as beautifully blue as a kingfisher. Her long dark hair seemed to belong to some lost noble tribe. Pierre had not seen much of her during her school year, although both their families were closely connected. Now it was time for her to be presented as one of the eligible young women in Parisian society. Her presence would be felt at the ball of the Comte de Paris, the old royalist sympathizer who told endless anecdotes to his audiences about the royal families of Europe.

The Comte's ball was to be held in the ballroom at Versailles, with its famous long gallery. Here it was rumored that the ghost of Louis XVI sometimes walked at night. Many of the noble families talked of such a legend. Accordingly the rooms were maintained, lest the royal ghosts of Marie and Louis might require a moment's pause in their restless voyage.

It was a well-established tradition that no one came to the ball at the hour stated. This ball reflected society at play. It was a human lottery. The final prize could be the gaining of the hand of an eligible partner. Many of those in attendance gorged themselves on everything the new, freshly-emerging city had to offer.

The Comte de Paris was a familiar figure, done up in a black frock coat and a large black silk hat. The Comte was not unaware of the satire which was heaped on his character, but he ignored these insults. He regarded his fellow ball goers as gross and slovenly in manner, and he made no bones about drawing attention to their garrulous behavior.

Even very demure ladies had to admit that they were aware of him. Indeed, the more he was gossiped about the less he remained a credible figure. It was rumored that he made up most of the stories about himself to gain notoriety. People needed to believe that he was a fabulous figure, larger than life. It would have been impossible for anyone to understand his magnificent personality.

The Long Gallery was an impressive room. The Gallery's windows caught the glorious sunset Corinthian pillars of green marble decorated its walls with seventeen arched windows looking out on the park. Facing the windows was a line of beveled mirrors, reflecting the view. The entire ceiling was painted with mythological scenes. On the south side of the room was a large area painted with river gods, and surrounded by nymphs. In their midst was the figure of Minerva, patroness of the arts, dispenser of wisdom, surrounded by the Muses.

The centre of the ceiling was a masterpiece, painted in lovely pinks and lavenders. The figures were delicate and graceful, and were wreathed round a large shell. The third and final section represented the goddess Venus, Deity of Love, failing in love with Adonis.

There were three glass Venetian chandeliers. Their red and blue lights seemed warm and eternally bathed in the glow of early summer. The statues of Diana the huntress and Venus de Milo served to embellish the ethereal beauty of the room. The Aubusson tapestry was shown to best effect in the fading light.

For the ball, Venetian eighteenth century costume had been adopted. The Comte de Paris preferred this masked ball to any other. The orchestra played Vivaldi, Corelli, Mozart and snatches of popular Venetian canzone.

A light breeze entered through the window. One could hear the lovely rustling sounds of silk dresses. They had sensuous shades of blue and green, and even watered silk, which seemed to whisper as it moved. The intricate movement of fans spoke a language of its own. The ladies had brought intricacy and subtlety to this art of calling, inviting, teasing and reflecting.

There was a criss-crossing in the various webs and patterns of conversation. The guests seemed like some superb scene from the painter David. What had begun as pools of sounds, some rising as strains from various corners swelled into a rush of water. The sound began to ebb and flow like the out-going tide. One could imagine the deities and the statues joining in the conversation.

***

It was possible only in one of the smaller drawing rooms to have any serious conversation. It was here that Pierre and Marie could talk to each other. He felt a desperate need for the tenderness of a woman, after all the years at the academy. With her intimacy and gentleness Marie had a way of showing that she understood him.

"I missed you so much", said Pierre.

"Me too ... even the letters you sent me made me more anxious to see you", replied Marie.

"Can I tell you something, Marie?"

"Of course."

"Can I tell it in complete confidence?"

"Of course, Pierre."

"My intention is to leave the Academy. I have had enough. I must inform my father and find another career."

"Do you dislike it so much? He will be angry, Pierre."

"He is always difficult," replied Pierre.

"You are right; there would be no pleasing him anyway. In his eyes you could never do the right thing. I'm so glad that you are not to become a soldier, Pierre", said Marie, displaying a deep compassion and affection that had first struck a chord in his young heart.

"But what will I do, Marie? Mother, I think, will be secretly pleased. You know how she always thought I should be a priest or teach at the university. She dislikes all the talk of battles and war. I don't want to belong to the academy any more. I do not want to stay there.

A strain of Vivaldi floated down as they entered a long mirror-lined corridor. They heard a melody that lulled and swayed in the air and broke the silence. Pierre stopped for a moment at a large oil painting that depicted a distinguished looking man in royal dress.

"Who is he?" questioned Marie.

"He is one of my ancestors, Julian Fredy. He was an officer."

"Has your family always been involved with the Royal Court of France?"

"We originally came from Italy in the fourteenth century", said Pierre.

"My father was a diplomat in Italy for many years. He lived near the French border, but the Germans took our land", replied Marie.

Marie and Pierre continued to walk down the corridor where they discovered a painting of Louis XIV, depicting him as Apollo and his family as Olympian gods.

"There he is ... Louis XIV, he believed himself to be Apollo", mused Pierre.

"Do you think he was a god?" asked Marie with a smile.

"Perhaps ... but the French no longer respect him or the aristocracy. That golden age is over." Pierre paused for a moment, and then turned to Marie." Forgive me", said Pierre.

"For what?" asked Marie, a little surprised.

"For pouring out all my problems to you", replied Pierre with a smile.

"It happens to me all the time", replied Marie.

"Marie, I do love you. Promise me you'll meet me in Paris soon", Pierre said, looking intently at her.

***

It was difficult for Pierre to imagine that his family had once been part of this history. How many kings and queens had walked these corridors, men and women with Europe at their feet? It was indeed an avenue of time.

Since his family had come to France in the fourteenth century, they had become part of this history. Pierre remembered that even his family name was acquired near Versailles in 1577, over three hundred years before. They had served the King of France in many ways: royal lawyers, judges, marshals of France, Royal Councilors, Commissioners of War, Treasurer Generals and Senior Councilors to parliament. It was Louis Xl who had ennobled the Fredys, when they came from Italy in March 1477; one of the family served him as chamberlain.

Francois Fredy, in the 17th century, belonged to the great court of Louis XIV. He acted as captain of the King's ships. But the family suffered the terrors of the French Revolution. Henri Louis de Coubertin was guillotined by the revolutionaries. Francois Louis survived narrowly, lost his title and took the name Citizen Fredy. It was due to the family's undying loyalty to the crown that the Bourbon King awarded Julien Bonaventure Fredy the Legion d'Honneur and gave him the hereditary title of Baron in 1821.

Pierre's mother was the daughter of Charles de Crisenoy and his wife Euphraise de Miraville. Pierre's maternal grandmother belonged to an ancient Norman family who had distinguished themselves as soldiers.

Pierre's legacy was deeply intertwined with the French royal family, a tradition that his father followed bravely even with the king in exile. What was he to do? He felt trapped in history; trapped in a tradition that he had no choice but to follow. He walked slowly along the corridor of mirrors and stood for a moment, looking at his reflection that echoed the past. How many ancestors of his had looked in these mirrors? He wrote in his diary, "How could I become a gentleman of the new world, imprisoned in the ruins of a dead past?" That was the way he felt, imprisoned in a past that for him no longer had any meaning within this New France, this New Republic. this New Europe. What was he to do with his life.

Pierre entered the throne room of Louis XIV, a room filled with extraordinary splendor. It was here that Francois Fredy, Captain of the King's ships, would have attended court to inform the King of events at sea. He imagined himself standing in the same spot amongst all those dignitaries and what it must have been like to belong to a court with all this pomp and power. It was here that the Sun King had sat and ruled his kingdom. But the revolution had come and France had found a new direction, a new ideal, a new republic. But he did not believe in violent revolutions. He wrote in his diary, on his return from Versailles, the feelings he had had there.

"From the tribune I cannot descend without falling ... the crowd no longer turns even with irritated glances... to stay up there counting the years and speaking of the old days and distrusting the future. But should I climb down, and separate ... from all my relatives by scandalizing them, should I listen to my father's pleadings... what then am I to do? Run away, and forget? But the hour for fleeing is past."

***

Gardens at Versailles

CHAPTER FOUR

PARIS 1887

Son of Kronos, master of windy Aitna,
Where powerful Typhos is trapped,
The hundred-headed,
Welcome an Olympian conqueror.

OLYMPIAN IV

Louis XIV
Pierre's father was a classical painter.He worked on drawings of sculptures in the louvres and painted religous pictures of thePope

The image of his father, Charles, returned to him. His strong will, his piercing eyes which glazed imperceptibly until the stare which at first seemed frightening became absorbed in the distance. They were the practiced eyes of a painter. Pierre remembered his gestures of the wrist, with a brush resting between the fingers and the thumb as the upward strokes were evenly applied to the canvas. At other times his movements were nervous and quick and he made a kind of instant flick of the fingers and then again they would become slow and patient.

His father worked on his canvas with a cool reasonable detachment, measured and controlled. His whole life moved between waking early, writing letters in the study, lunch and rest. He approached everything in a formal and respectful manner, he was urbane and charming. Everything was spoken in a matter of fact way, the only dramatic gesture was the arching of his eyebrows in agreement. Pierre recalled his porcelain eyes, with the light blue glaze of ducks' eggs that gave the only indication of intelligence and alertness.

It was easy to forget his father; in the previous years he had become almost a recluse. His work celebrating sublime moments of the history of France continued, with themes of lost symbols of an age. For twenty years he had painted. It was a life dedicated to this obsession. Charles had said that the past survived within these old paintings, recording the deeds of mankind, its conflicts and celebrations. But his work was not a mere fossil or a reflection of a society; it reminded each generation of the scenes of faith and valor.

The torch of faith was handed from one generation to the next, and it was rekindled and kept burning from the simple noble love of the faithful. Thus, the Church had survived the early persecutions; the faith of the fathers lived on.

In a certain sense Charles was locked between two rooms; they were his private domain, a solitary place of his making, filled with engravings and books on the history of the world.

Each day he evoked the great images of the Church as he worked on his paintings. The house was homage to geometry, built in a classical style. It was a house which had already become a museum. All the granite was cut back to conform to it principle of bygone aesthetics. Tapestry work and pattern dominated the whole place; even the walls were perfectly smooth with their limestone pattern. Everything was for the pleasure of the eye. Charles could look out on the small enclosure of land, and from it project an image of larger gardens that equally pleased the eye. For him there was no concession to any idea of disorder.

At the end of the day, Charles could sit there, when the weather permitted, and derive from the exactness of the place the most indescribable emotions of pleasure. He loved to think that one could live two lives, the one that was common to every one from birth to death, and the other which the artist must pursue.

Pierre had almost forgotten his father's existence. He had been requested to meet him in the library, to discuss his future. It was it formal interview in which Pierre would be questioned. Returning again to the library, he was paying a visit to his own past.

It was clear now why his father had painted as he had, living in a country in which he was profoundly unhappy. The paintings of the various Roman scenes and of the Papal Mass, the death of saintly priests, of a Roman Cardinal, were themes chosen not because of their grandeur but as a way of refusing to acknowledge the present. He had created many paintings with glorious themes. The discovery of the Lagoon, Rome 1506, hung in the salon in 1846. Promenades of a Roman Cardinal, 1857. The Pontifical Cortege, 1861. The Martyr's last Mass, 1864. Charles celebrated the glories of the Church. He was a painter creating work that was losing an audience. Parisians wanted to see the works of Courbet's 'The Bathers' or Manet's 'Olympia'. But no matter what effort was made to make the new regimes acceptable, no matter how they might hope to earn respectability, they could be resisted by these paintings full of reference to the classical past, to the Church, to his own family and to scenes from French history. Charles was making a memory in oil, which helped deny the new claims being made every day. The last effort of a proud and powerless man!

His father's constant talk about the state of France resulted in Pierre's sensitivity to the message of silver coins. In Pierre's pocket one could find three monarchies, two empires and three republics, all from the coins that were in circulation from the past eighty years. France was indeed a country of too many revolutions!

When he entered the library he found his father there, standing at one of the shelves which ran parallel to the windows facing north, making this room, with windows in this position, suitable for reading. Both rooms were full of cool, calm light. It was from this room that his father worked. He was tall and imposing as he turned to greet Pierre.

"Good morning, Pierre. You remember this book; it is a history of Byzantium. I believe it was the favorite book of his Majesty, Louis XIV, and the life of the court was based on it. I have been speaking with your mother. All the reports on your conduct agree that you have been exemplary in your life at the Academy. It is a great satisfaction to us both that you and Albert have chosen to serve France in this way.

You know how many of our ancestors distinguished themselves in the service of the army, so we are glad to see the family tradition continued."

It was the coolness and control of exchange that could not be forgotten; what Charles said-the tenor of the voice, the inclination of the head, the strength with which the eyes gazed upon you with absolute conviction.

"I'm not altogether sure that the life at St Cyr is what I want, father," Pierre said quite painfully, saying more than he had intended.

"What do you mean?"

"Well, I must say it is upon much deliberation and thought that I have come to a decision to leave the Academy."

"Leave the Academy! Pierre! That is impossible! ... It will be a disgrace to all of us. You have excellent reports. But why, Pierre, are you unhappy for a particular reason?"

"No father ... I cannot find any meaning in this study ... I do not have a vocation for military life."

It had been in that one sentence which he could recall perfectly that Pierre had boldly taken revenge on his father. It was also in that one sentence that he had accepted the impossibility of their ever speaking to each other again. Conversation was a strain at the best of times. It was always the same theme, and Charles was never vulnerable because he could assert the same set of inconvertible propositions: the Pope, the State, and the infallibility of the absolute.

Moments of silence passed since Pierre had spoken. It was a' memory most painful even to recall. As he looked at his father, he did not see the broad figure that was there when he first entered; before him now stood a man tired with age and doomed to disappointment.

As he stood there with his arms crossed, he resembled only the picture of sadness. Pierre realized now that it was no longer possible to struggle with his father any longer.

Lake at Versailles
Pierre and Marie often walked in the park
in their ancestors footsteps

CHAPTER FIVE

ENGLAND 1893

Yet we can in greatness of mind
Or of body be like the Immortals,
Tho' we know not to what goal
By day or in the nights
Fate has written that we shall run.

NEMEAN VI

The English Olympic Games
Pierre travelled from Normandy to Much Wenlock in
Shropshire to meet with the local Dr Brookes
It was Brookes who gave him the idea to revive the games

ENGLAND 1893

Travel was the way he had escaped his father. It seemed that all Pierre's journeys were an escape from him. It was to England he travelled, a country now changed totally by the Industrial Revolution. The idea of exile was appealing, and the chance to find a new path in his life.

The pointed shore curved sharply and fell away from the cliff, descending to a harbor in which boats were invisible. Flocks of gulls rode the wind in a lazy, gliding motion. They tipped their wings, climbing suddenly upwards until they were against the cliffs, like silent acrobats who played between shore and sea. The wind had captured them as they followed the boat. They soared upwards towards the land and out of sight.

Pierre heard the sounds of passengers and orders from the ship's crew to disembark. The journey was over. He had a sense of nervous relief. Impatiently he waited for the gangplank to be lowered.

He could see beyond beautiful woods. This new shoreline gave him a feeling of profound peace. For the first time he knew he had found a kind of liberty, as he stared off into the distance at the rolling hills.

***

The train took him north to Shropshire to the Comte's house. The steam belched from the great funnel, and its sharp whistle pierced the still air of the countryside.

He began to think of the Comte. He had not seen him since the great ball at Versailles. Yes, his father was right; the Comte was indeed an eccentric. He had lived a lavish lifestyle in Paris, womanizing, and throwing banquets. He had always believed in the return of the King. Like Pierre's father he was a confirmed royalist and no lover of the new republic. He had left France disillusioned with the end of the royal order.

Pierre had heard rumors about the Comte. Occasionally someone would return from across the Channel and talk of the varying collection of people, artists, poets and writers that the Comte invited to his villa. It was a salon one could compare to a menagerie of exotic and wonderful birds.

He had learned something of England from his reading of the book, Tom Brown's Schooldays. It described a young English boy's days at Rugby School. He had read about this college where Thomas Arnold had evoked the ideas of the ancient schools of Sparta in Greece.

As he travelled northwards he began to notice the change in the landscape, blighted by the new industrial revolution. The houses huddled around giant chimneys made of red brick; smoke belched out from these giant stacks. What had happened to England, he wondered?

***

He arrived at a small station near the village of Wenlock where he took a carriage to the Comte's house. At the end of the tree-lined avenue a large Palladian house came into view. Pierre observed great marble pillars with sweeping white steps that ran down to a fountain beside a statue of Venus. He saw the figure of the Comte approaching him. Pierre stepped out of the carriage and one of the Comte's servants took his bags. The Comte stood before him wearing a long, crimson seventeenth century coat and leather knee boots. He beamed a great smile."Oh, Pierre, mon cheri, it's so good to see you." said the Comte, putting his arms around him.

"It's good to see you, too," laughed Pierre, relieved to see him. They entered the baroque interior of a sprawling country house. The house was in disrepair, filled with classical furniture, statues of Apollo and paintings scattered about the rooms and lying at random, unpacked. The Comte approached a golden throne beside a marble fireplace and motioned Pierre to take a seat.

"Now, tell me, Pierre, I believe you have been having a rough time in Paris," said the Comte, pouring some wine.

"Yes, my father was furious at my decision to leave the academy," replied Pierre, taking a chair.

"Well, Charles always wanted his children to do their duty. Your brothers, Albert and Paul, what are they up to?"

"One is in the army and the other is in the Papal Guard," replied Pierre.

"And your sister, Marie?" "She is studying music."

"Charles must be furious with you."

"But he does what he wants to do. He paints."

"Yes, he's interested in history too, Pierre, family history ... You have to play the game ...I don't agree with all this rubbish about duty, myself."

"He's threatened to wipe me out of the family inheritance," said Pierre despondently.

"Who cares, Pierre? You already have your share of it ... You can become a playboy or a vagabond. Have you a young lady?"

"Yes, her name's Marie."

"A woman will do you good. I have a mistress at present," said the Comte, draining his glass swiftly.

Before the words had left his lips, Pierre observed a young lady standing at the doorway, looking intently. He could see her from the corner of his eye. She had a face like an angel. It was rounded almost like a cherub. She had bright blue eyes and fair hair which seemed to shimmer in light and cast a halo around her head. He heard the rustling of her dress and observed this beautiful creature crossed the room.

"Oh, Natalie, come here. I want you to meet Pierre. He has just arrived from Paris."

"Delighted to meet you. You must be exhausted," said Natalie, extending her hand.

"Natalie has recently come from Paris. She's studying archaeology at the Sorbonne."

"Do you plan on returning to France?" enquired Pierre.

"No, she's staying here with me," said the Comte.

"Surely you want to return some day," said Natalie.

"Not at all," replied the Comte.

"He wants to see a King on the throne again," Natalie said. "He hates the republic."

"Yes, they took so much away from us ... they have robbed us of our history, our culture, our symbols, our spirit ... but now I think it's even time to leave England," said the Comte.

"But why?" asked Pierre.

"Come with me, Pierre," said the Comte, beckoning them.

The Comte got up from his throne and they walked towards the French windows into the garden, followed by Natalie. He pointed to the horizon.

"You can see all that smoke, all those black chimneys?"

"He is always talking like this, Pierre," said Natalie, putting her arms around the Comte.

"They are destroying the beauty God gave us ... what can we do? This Industrial Revolution is like the black plague. The people no longer believe in their God, in nature or in the spirit ... this house has become a refuge for such men ... occultists, writers ... those who believe in fighting this horrific revolution," bellowed the Comte.

"Let me get Doctor Brooke. He's awake now," said Natalie, making her way to the drawing room?
"Who is Doctor Brooke," Pierre asked.
"He's an old friend from a village near Wenlock. A doctor... but his great dream is to revive the Olympics," answered the Comte.

"The Olympics ... the Greek Olympics?" replied Pierre.
"Exactly," said the Comte.
"Where?" asked Pierre."
"In England. We have had an Olympic festival... on the estate here ... but he has a grander ambition, on a very large scale ...

but he's very old now, Pierre, he's just an old man with a dream."

***

Some minutes later, Pierre heard footsteps behind him. He turned and observed an old, rather rail man holding a walking stick. Natalie held his arm. Dr. Brooke was the man who had dreamed of Olympism all his life and had carried the ideal faithfully. His face was framed by a Victorian beard which cut along his jaw line. It was his eyes which first caught Pierre's attention; steely blue eyes that had an eternal gaze about them. He noticed the frail bony hands clutching a walking stick. There was something dignified about the man, a kind of nobility that came with age.

"This is Dr Brooke," said Natalie, helping him forward.

"Delighted to meet you," said Pierre, shaking his frail hand.

"A pleasure, my boy," said Dr Brooke.

"The Comte has just told me of your noble ambition," replied Pierre.

"It is a wonderful idea, Pierre, of reviving the Games and the sacred flame of peace," said Natalie enthusiastically.

"The sacred flame!" Pierre echoed.

"The sacred flame was first lit at Olympia in Greece. All wars ceased when the Games started. They ended over fifteen hundred years ago. My dream is to re-light it", said Dr. Brooke, raising his right arm.

"Have you had any support for this great project?" asked Pierre.
"Very little from the government. I have tried in a small way in this village of Wenlock ... Alas, I'm now getting too old, Pierre.
"Nonsense, Dr Brooke, you still have fire in you!"

"No, Pierre, you're very kind, but I'm very tired and too old for, all this now. Every year the support dwindles ... it's like the Church ... the young ones are in the cities now ... we are forgetting our past."

"Why is it so important to you?"

"We need these great traditions ... This sacred truce was so powerful!"

***

Dr. Brooke's eyes lit up. Pierre observed a little boy, galloping along on a white horse and blowing a trumpet, approach the house. He wore a Grecian costume and his long, blonde hair trailed in the wind.

"Who is this boy?" asked Pierre, quite surprised.

"He's our mascot, Tom Yeats," replied Dr. Brooke

."Mascot?"

"Our mascot for the Olympic Games. His bugle call announces their opening every year."

"What a wonderful idea," exclaimed Pierre.

The young boy on the white steed approached them, bringing his white horse to a halt.

"I come in the name of Apollo. I have a letter for you, Dr. Brooke."

The little boy dismounted from his horse, tied it to the railings and hurried towards the doctor.

"Oh Tom, you are wonderful", said Natalie kissing him warmly. "Where is the letter from?"

"It's from Greece, it's got the royal stamp of the King."" The King of Greece?" said Pierre, surprised.

Dr. Brooke opened the letter. Pierre observed a flood of emotion in Dr Brooke's face.
"The King of Greece sends his regards. He has agreed to award gold medals for the next Shropshire Olympic Games."

***

Pierre and the Comte retired to his drawing room with his guests. They spoke all evening of a dying era. The Comte had recently become a member of a secret society called the Golden Circle. This was a secret occult group. Its aim was the revival of ancient spiritualistic practices and pagan cultures throughout the Western world. But its members hoped to dig much further into the past. They wished to explore the subconscious. They believed they could contact a mythical consciousness through talking to the spirits. These occult practices were new to Pierre. After all, his family was Catholic and disapproved of pagan practices.

The Comte believed that ancient gods might emerge from 'the great gates of the mountains.' He had had visions of ghostlike forms from the past since he had come to England. The Comte talked passionately of his visions of floating figures. He claimed to have seen them. He related how he was once greeted by the ghost of Louis XIV. The King was holding the bloodied head of a guillotined royalist, and the victim's hands were covered in blood.

***

Pierre spoke for many hours with Dr. Brooke, who began to fill him in on the history of attempts to revive Olympism in Europe. He was fascinated to discover that twenty years earlier Oscar Wilde had walked across the plains of Olympia. He had travelled there with Professor Mahaffy of the Classics Department of Trinity College Dublin. They too had gone in search of that sacred place. Dr. Brooke recalled how they had attended the Zappian Games of 1875. There Mahaffy and Wilde met with the King of Greece on the 15th February. They spoke with the King of a great Hellenic revival, and the Ancient Games.

"You are not the first one that has tried to relight the flame," said Pierre, tugging on the pockets of his waistcoat and looking across the lawns of Much Wenlock.

"The Romans brought their own games to England. There were some Games in Ireland too," said Doctor Brooke.

"The Olympian Games?"

"No - but something quite similar-the Tailteann Games with chariot and foot races, poetry, music and a sacred truce."

"The sacred truce!" exclaimed Pierre.

"Yes, they had the sacred truce there too, in Ireland under Brehon law. Death was the penalty for breaking it.' You know, they say the Irish are in fact Greeks."

"Greeks?"

"Yes, Greeks. The ancient tribes who invaded Ireland came from Greece."

"Irish gold work closely resembles Greek gold work of that time."

"When did the Games die out in Ireland?"

"In 1172. They went on longer than the Greek Games, which ended in the sixth century. Another six hundred years."

"Do you think it is possible to revive these Games?"

"My son, anything is possible if you believe in it. The time has come for another revival of these ancient beliefs. It's like a great wave coming over the horizon. Somehow those ancient men with chariots still linger in skies, like the seven horsemen of the Apocalypse."

***

Dr. Brooke took Pierre across the cricket lawns of Much Wenlock to the pavilion. There they talked all afternoon. For the first time, Pierre realized that he was gripped by Olympic fever. Dr. Brooke spoke about the great myths of Greece and the heroic ideal. That was the human condition, to struggle with surmounting our problems and to seek deliverance in our lives. The human spirit, for all its darker forces, was in essence heroic. The wise old doctor held Pierre's attention with his Olympic tales.

Dr. Brooke told how the revived Olympic ideal was first sown in Greece by Prince Otto of Bavaria. He had become King of the Hellenes and had proposed the revival of the Games in 1837, issuing a decree that sporting events including discus, javelin, long jump, footraces, chariot racing, and wrestling should be held. But this proposal came to nothing.

"In 1854 a Greek writer named Soutos published an article in a national newspaper suggesting the revival of the Games. Thi suggestion was read by a Greek millionaire, Evangelis Zappas, who was so taken by the idea that he wrote to King Otto, offering the finance for the proposed Games in 1856. Otto turned to his foreign minister, Dr. Ramjaves for advice.

Although a classicist, this cabinet minister was lukewarm in his support. But the enthusiastic Zappas would take no objections. He consulted architects and was given an estimate of one million drachmas.Three years later the Games took place at Freedom Square in Athens. The celebrations were disturbed by the collapse of the 1,500 meters winner, who subsequently died. In 1865 Zappas died leaving a fortune, which was to ensure that the modern Games would take place every four years. In his will he stipulated that the stadium should continue to be re-built and marble seating should be added. His final request was that his body was to be buried in a Rumanian church, and his head, cut from his body, be buried in Athens. These wishes were complied with, and a plaque was added at the Athenian burial place, bearing the words:

'HERE LIES THE HEAD OF EVANGELIS ZAPPAS'.

In 1870 there was the 2nd Olympiad. The committee of that year spent 200,000 drachmas on the Games. But unfortunately Zappas's will was not carried out by the trustees as he had planned. The last attempted revival of the Olympics was the Panhellenic games in 1891, which did not achieve the scale hoped for."Dr. Brooke spoke too of the early seeds of the idea in Europe. "Perhaps the earliest suggestion was in 1793 a German named Guttas-Muths suggested the idea.

In Sweden, Professor Schartan of the University of Lund organized a festival at Ramlosa in 1834 in honor of the ancient Olympic Games, and a second Scandinavian Olympic Games in 1836.

***

Pierre sat back in his chair. He continued to listen to Dr. Brooke. He began to realize that the time he would spend in England would become condensed into the memory of that village with the peculiar sounding name of Much Wenlock, situated twelve miles from Shrewsbury and forty miles to the west of Birmingham. About twelve hundred years previously a royal abbey had stood there. Around the same date the games had ceased in Olympia. Much Wenlock was a place where time had stood still. A sense of antiquity clung to its landscape.

It was in this landscape that Dr. Brooke had attended the sick and too often watched his people die. Pierre realized that he had a feeling of deep affection for this old man. He noted the doctor's impressive eyes, which looked with such compassion on those who had suffered. He had weather-beaten features, making him appear ageless. Pierre observed these rugged features, the thin broad mouth, the straying grey hair, the firm creased hands strong with character and filled with experience. Brooke spoke of peace and the practice of love. He knew that without an ideal there was nothing in this life.

Dr. Brooke's room was small, full of bric-a-brac and heavy old furniture. The dresser was packed with commemorative plates and trophies. On the walls were pictures of fox hunting and landscapes by unknown artists. They sat opposite each other at a small table laden with cakes and tea. It was the perfect afternoon. It was the hour before the sun begins to set. Taking tea was an exemplary ritual in a country which made a ceremony of greeting and parting. Pierre, however, had sensed that the doctor's invitation was more than a simple diversion.

Dr. Brooke took out a heavily bound album encased in tanned leather. At the middle of the cover stamped in gold, was the title 'Wenlock Olympia', surrounded by Greek decorations. The large brass clasp was like that on a family bible. The heavy boards had beveled edges which opened back to reveal all the proceedings of his society. Pierre observed one memo in particular: it was a petition to the English parliament in 1867 to revive the Games. Another letter in 1881 recorded his request for 'An International Olympian Festival to be held in Athens'. He gestured to Pierre to come closer and have a look. They sat for an hour whilst Dr. Brooke read and explained what had been taking place for over forty years. It had been his whole life, the meaning of his existence.

Then Dr. Brooke got up and opened one of his giant cabinets. He took the most beautiful cup from the glass case.

"I have something else to show you, Pierre. I think of this cup as a symbol. The dream of reviving the Games and uniting them with the spirit of Olympia has been inspired by this chalice, this sacred cup. It is a kind of Holy Grail. You understand, Pierre, a holy grail?"

Pierre learned that the sacred cup had come from the King of Greece as a gift. It seemed to glow in the room. For Dr. Brooke it was a religious symbol. Dr. Brooke lapsed into a quiet smile, and it seemed as if the golden cup was dissolving in the evening light. It had become an object with an extraordinary presence. Dr. Brooke seemed to Pierre like a child absorbed, inhabiting the world of his dreams.

"Dear Pierre,
That was the original reason for the Games. I began my little

games on February 25th 1850. I wanted to promote the moral, physical and intellectual improvement of the people of Wenlock. I wanted to help especially the poorer classes."

He went on to explain that there had been an attempted revival in England before by Robert Dover, who started the Cotswold Olympics in 1636. There bands had marched, cannons fired, teams competed and bonfires and fireworks lit up the evening sky. Then a torch light procession was made to the town square. Brooke informed Pierre of another attempted revival in London, Chelsea in 1838 and held at the stadium in the grounds of Cremorne House on the banks of the Thames by the owner, Baron de Berenger.

Dr. Brooke went on to tell his story. He was born in Much Wenlock in 1809, the son of a doctor. He had studied medicine in London and Paris and followed in his father's footsteps.

When his father died of typhoid in 1830 he returned to his home town to take over his practice. It was perhaps due to his awareness of the physical condition of the people and the diseases, such as typhoid and cholera, that Dr. Brooke was prompted to revive the Games on a small scale. He told Pierre that once on his way to Paris he had found a book in an inn about Huguenot weavers who had died out in the third generation, due to the exploitation in the giant industrial mills.

People had been taken away from their natural environment. Inside huge brick buildings, men and women toiled away from dawn to dusk. What was the point of this Industrial Revolution, Pierre wondered despairingly, unless it helped the progress of mankind?

Dr. Brooke described the events of his Shropshire Olympics, begun in 1850. These were held on the rolling plains of Wenlock in a place known as the Linden Fields. Hundreds of people assembled beside a gaily colored grandstand and marquee. There, the young mascot Tom Yeats sounded his trumpet, mounted on a white horse, and galloped across the open fields declaring the Games open. Tom was dressed in a sixteenth century costume, recalling images from Arthurian legend.

The contestants wore medieval costume and carried Olympic banners with Greek inscriptions. The winners were presented with laurel crowns. The medals were stamped with the image of the Maltese Cross enclosed in a wreathed medallion. Some of the medals had the image of the winged goddess Nike, goddess of victory, inscribed on them. Dr. Brooke had corresponded with the King of Greece who had sent medals to be awarded at the Zappian Olympic Games in 1859. The King had sent him prizes also in 1877. Dr. Brooke founded the Shropshire Olympian Society in 1861 and the National Olympian Association in 1865.

"What's so special about Olympia?" questioned Pierre.

"Olympia was dedicated to sport. The Greeks celebrated the Olympic Games at Olympia, uninterrupted for over a thousand years," replied Dr. Brooke.

"Why did they stop?"

"It was a pagan festival that was ended by the Christian Roman emperor Theodosius in 392A. D. It was really war which ended the Games. War broke out between Athens and Sparta about 400.B.C. which lost them their neutral status, thereby weakening the value of the Olympic oath. There was a time when peace was sacred, when men believed in a truce that was so valuable that it was respected by all of the Greeks. So, when the Games were in progress all wars throughout Greece ceased, for a month. At the announcement of the Games, soldiers threw down their shields and put away their arms."

"A sacred truce of peace. Now it is all forgotten." Pierre said sadly.

"Yes, Pierre, you know the King of Belgium once said, 'It takes twenty years of peace to make a man. It takes only twenty seconds of war to destroy him.'"

***

Brooke informed him of archaeological discoveries, which paralleled the development of the Games in Greece. Around 1870 there was much research into the Homeric myths and the Olympic Games. George Grote, an English historian, believed that there was a sharp distinction between legendary and historical Greece. Greek history began for him with the first Olympiad in 776 B.C.

In 1858 William Gladstone put forward the argument that the Trojan War was an historical event. This was discredited by contemporary classical historians. But a German explorer, Heinrich Schliemann, was destined to rediscover Troy. He had boyhood dreams of ancient Greece, which haunted him and became his great passion. It was in 1870 that he set off to the Troad in Turkey, where the ancient city of Troy was believed to be buried. There after many months of digging, myth became reality. Troy and the treasure of King Priam was discovered.

Schliemann wrote to King George of Greece on the day of his great discovery.

'To His Majesty King George of the Hellenes. With extreme joy, I announce to your Majesty that I have discovered the tombs of Agamemnon and Cassandra. This is the place where the hand some Paris and fair Helen landed in their flight from Sparta. When I discovered this site I was filled with an intense desire to begin digging, and lay bare for the world the city of Priam, and the war recorded by Homer.'

***

"Well, if the King of Greece supports you, there should not be a problem," said Pierre.

"Well, it's extremely difficult, this revival. There's a man named Gennadius, the Greek Charge d'Affaires in London, who keeps me informed. He tells me I will find a very sympathetic audience in Greece. Pierre, I'm an old man now; eighty two years old to be precise. I have not the energy for such a great idea. I've spent forty years trying to revive the Games on a national scale. But it is difficult."

"It is such a noble and wonderful idea," replied Pierre.

"You're a young man, Pierre You have youth on your side. Perhaps we have met here for a special reason, Pierre. The years given to a man are numbered. There is not much time left for me. I have written pamphlets and sent letters. But they have been ignored. Recently Mr. Gennadius from the Greek Embassy has written to me. He thinks we English are impossible romantics. We have lost the passion of Byron and
the understanding of the ancient ways. Look at us, Pierre; our culture has been made in Athens and in Rome. In Athens we once saw the light, in the poems and works of Pindar, Plato and Socrates. Study them well, Pierre. It is the spirit of man, of our whole world. In the cities of London and Paris we must rebuild the worship of this learning of the mind and of freedom. Even the very basis of our democracy was invented by the Greeks."
Dr. Brooke continued; "We are now beginning to crush man in

these factories and destroy his dignity. Think, Pierre, in Olympia they read poetry, played music and competed in sports. Everyone from Shepherd to King deemed it an honor to come to that sacred place. They gave truth, vigor and perfection to the Games. It would wonderful, Pierre if, after almost two thousand years, the Games could be revived! The sacred truce observed and once again the ideal could be brought back to life. Then the sacred flame could be re-lit and peace would once again be observed at Olympia. You could revive this history again and remake the past and revive it. It would not be like some old pageant but it would bring back and reaffirm the genius of the Greeks, and bring forward the day when man would become complete."

Dr. Brooke's large-lidded brown eyes rested on the cup, and then the album. Only then did the tolling of the village church bell remind Pierre of how much time had passed. Brooke lifted his eyes and looked at Pierre.

"Pierre, can I ask you something? A simple request?"

"Certainly."

"I sense that my time in this world is very short. Will you continue my work; at least understand the spirit of it? Perhaps some day you can make it possible," said Dr. Brooke, taking the sacred cup, kissing it and handing it to Pierre.

"I would like you to have this, Pierre. It was the sacred cup given to me by the King of Greece. It once held the oil that lit the sacred flame at Olympia. If you ever find somebody worthy to give this cup to, hand it on."

Pierre smiled and took the cup and wondered if he could one day complete his vision, and give back to Greece its ancient Games.

Only the candle flickered now at the centre of the round table. Dr. Brooke clutched his chair. Pierre could hear the slow, barely perceptible breathing of the Doctor. His face was like a sculpture in this candlelight. Dr. Brooke appeared to be in a trance. The room was filled with an intense silence.

Dr. Brooke spoke softly." Will you help me in my quest ... to revive the ancient games? Men no longer believe in the ancient ways ... we must preserve the ancient rituals ..."

Then his voice wavered as if floating through time, echoing slightly ..."Someone must carry the sacred flame of Olympia ... someone must take up the quest. We must continue this ancient ritual ... we must convince men and nations of its possibility."

"Preserve the flame, Pierre... preserve the flame. Keep watch on the sacred flame."

Then Dr. Brooke's voice stopped, as quickly as it had echoed into the darkness. A powerful silence seemed to enter the room. The candle wavered on the table. It would he forty years later before Pierre would realize the significance of this moment.

That night Pierre could not sleep. He lay in the darkness without fear. The peace of sleep did not come easily. The summer's night had cooled down and the dawn approached. From his room in Wenlock he could reflect on his life and look across to the small lake to where the sun would rise soon beyond the hills. Pierre reflected on the beautiful charm of Dr. Brooke's old age, his modest personality, and his great dream. Dr Brooke's ideal was a last innocent attempt to stop England's decay.

In the years when George II sat on the throne, the face of England had changed forever. Hamlets had grown rapidly into towns. Chimneys bellowing with smoke rose into the sky, to compete with ancient church spires. Hundreds of houses were built back to back to accommodate the new working classes. The poor could no longer smell the country air. They huddled beneath these spires, toiling from dawn till dusk.

Dr. Brooke had observed the growth of these towns and the destruction of village life, where the youth traveled to the big cities in search of work. It was a revolution that brought death on a grand scale, where a great many toiled in such squalid conditions. Even children were made to slave away in factories and mines.

Dr. Brooke had tried in his own way to protect his people. He believed that the only way of fighting this exploitation was by keeping up their strength. From his small cottage window he observed daily yet another coffin being brought to the cemetery at Wenlock. Such was the industrial machine which was to affect the lives of millions. The villagers were thankful if God had spared them and if death had not claimed them before the age of thirty five.

Dr. Brooke's outlook echoed in Pierre's writings at this time.
"If we begin to study the history of our century we are struck by the moral disorder produced by the discoveries of industrial science. Life suffers an upheaval; people feel the ground tremble continually under their feet. They have nothing to hold on to, because everything around them is shifting and changing; and in their confusion, as though seeking some counterpoise to the material powers which rise like Cyclopean ramparts about them, they grope for whatever elements of moral strength lie scattered about the world. I think this is the philosophic origin of the striking physical renaissance in the nineteenth century."

Pierre pondered these facts. He considered the value of Brooke's ideal. Perhaps it was not just a romantic idea, but a practical solution. It was an idea that had a power all of its own. Pierre reflected that by recreating the Olympic ideal one could challenge the future. He was beginning to realize that here was a quest worth fighting for.

In England and Ireland the great Olympian ideal had existed and lingered on for over a thousand years. Here too the spirit of Olympia had been preserved. Now it was time for a new revival. New Olympians dreamt of an Olympic revival. It occurred to Pierre that out there beneath the stars other men might be dreaming the same dream. How could one forge links between these men? Would Dr. Brooke's knowledge and beliefs follow him to the grave? Who would carry the torch? There was a germ, Pierre knew, of a great movement.

His mind returned again to Paris. Marie was thinking of him. He was so pleased to receive a letter one morning from her, delivered by Tom Yeats from the village.

"My Dear Pierre,

"I think of you always. Even at this latest hour! I dream of you and your sweet smile. I wonder if you are lonely or feeling the way I do, longing for you. Running away won't solve anything. You can not run away from yourself. Sometimes I wonder what drives you. Why are you so restless? Why are you in search of something? Oh, Pierre, I wish you were here now. The light streams through my window and across the pages of my diary. I imagine your hand touching mine. I only realize now my true emotions for you when you are so far away.

"All my love,

"Marie."

Before Pierre returned to France Dr Brooke suggested that he visit Rugby College.

Pierre had read about the great work of Thomas Arnold and the reform of the English Public School system. Arnold had been appointed headmaster in 1828. He successfully regenerated the school to the same level as Eton and Winchester.

Arnold introduced history, mathematics and modern history .He modernized the teaching of the classics by directing attention to literary, moral and historical questions. He had a deep sympathy for the poor and in 1831 he started a newspaper that advocated social reform. In 1841 Arnolds was appointed Regius professor of modern history in Oxford but he died suddenly in 1842. His life and work became immortalized in Stanley's Life and Correspondence and Thomas Hughes novel Tom Browns Schooldays.

Pierre traveled to Rugby deep in thought with his time with Dr Brooks. The playing field, green lush, spread before him. He walked with the Dean through the grounds of Rugby met with pupils and learnt of their team sports.

But alone he entered the church at Rugby College .Alone he sat in the great vaulted aisle .The light streamed through the stained glass windows ,colours spread by a prism; gold, red, blue. An organ player tested his fingers before service. As the music soared upwards, he felt that this was the turning point of his life. This idea of Brookes about reviving the Olympic Games was a beautiful one, a spiritual quest that would engage his life, a heroic quest to revive ideals long dead and lost. At that moment he was seized by a vision to of games for all men whatever the colour or race .A games to promote world peace, a games made in the spirit of love and co-operation.
At that moment he knew that there was no turning back he would make his mark on history.

***

Tom Yates, Mascot of the Much Wenlock Olympian Society
He holds the cup sent by the King of Greece

SIX

PARIS 1893

Welcome from him this rite of crowns and choir,
Which he brings from the plain of Pisa,
Victor in the foot-race and the Five Events together;
He has won what no mortal man has won before.

OLYMPIAN VII

The Marathon Cup Given to Loues by The King of Greece
Dr Brookes was sent a similar cup by the King
who he regularly corresponded with from his tiny hamlet
in Shropshire

Pierre's sleepless nights continued on his return from England. He awoke in his cabin late at night, and observed the sacred cup gleaming gold and blue in the moonlight. What was he to do? Should he take up a dying man's request, or cast it aside? Should he vow to undertake this sacred mission? The time had come to make a decision. What was he to do with his life? Here was a sacred cup, the emblem of an ancient religion. Here was an ideal waiting to be fulfilled.

Pierre wrote in his diary: "...and for the Olympic Games which modern Greece has not yet revived, it is not a Greek to whom one is indebted but rather to Dr. W.P.Brookes ... now aged 82 ... still active, vigorous, organizing and animating them ... Athletics does not count many partisans as convinced as Dr. W.P.Brookes."

The idea of sacrifice had occupied Pierre's mind since he had read his uncle's diary. He reflected that a man is capable of sacrificing everything in the quest of his ideals. A man can go against his own self-interest. In a world obsessed by greed Pierre had discovered that one could still devote one's life to humanity. When a man acts in this way he can bring about fundamental changes in the lives of others. Pierre had begun to understand that there were men who selflessly pursed an ideal for the greater good of mankind. Dr. Brooke had pursued this belief all his life. The Christian ideal of love had lost its popularity in the industrial wastelands of this new revolution. Nobody asked for self-sacrifice. It was a lost value in this new world.

This was the dilemma that existed in a rapidly changing world. Pierre realized that he too could become a part of this dilemma. What had changed him in England? Was it just coincidence, a casual meeting that had changed his life? Pierre returned to France with much on his mind. In a way, Dr. Brooke had politely handed over his life's work. Now Pierre was trying to understand the significance of this. What was he to do with an ancient cult that had been dead for over a thousand years?

***

Marie was waiting for him at the Gare du Nord. She hurried along the platform in a long blue coat and a feathered hat.

"Oh , Pierre, I've missed you. I thought you would come back sooner. How was your trip?" said Marie, out of breath.

"Marie, it was wonderful ... I've missed you, so much," said Pierre, throwing his arms around her and kissing her.

They took a carriage to a nearby restaurant and sat beneath a mosaic dome.

"So how are you, Marie? What have you been up to?

"I've been to my parents' house by the sea at Combray and to the tailors to get some new dresses made. But Pierre, tell me! What was the Comte like?"

"Oh, he's very eccentric. He has a young mistress. He hates France. But now he's beginning to hate England."

"But why?"

"Because he says its spirit is dying, since the Industrial Revolution began. They are building these monstrous factories, where hundreds of people toil in dirt and grime every day for a few pennies. Even children have to work."
"Children! Oh, my God. The poor things."

"Yes, they are leaving the countryside in their thousands. They are losing their past, their identities. They no longer believe in the old ways, in their myths and their folklore. I have met a fascinating man at the Comte's house. He talks of reviving the immortal spirit of Olympia. He believes that the ancient Olympics have a power about them. If the sacred flame is lit it will help to revive the spirit of an age that is dying. He believes it to be a new kind of religion," explained Pierre.

"Have you any plans for the future?" questioned Marie.

"Yes, I have been giving it much thought while I was in England. I don't want to be in the army any more, I don't want to become a boring old bureaucrat. I'm going to do something with my life, something worthwhile, something important." said Pierre, opening the box which held the sacred cup.

"It's beautiful! It's wonderful! What is it?" said Marie, excitedly.

"It is the sacred cup which held the oil that re-lit the flame at Olympia. Dr Brooke gave it to me."

Marie looked at Pierre intently. Then she kissed him softly.

"I missed you, Pierre, while you were away," said Marie, kissing him again.

"I felt the same way, Marie," said Pierre holding her hand.

"Is your father still angry?"

"I do not care what my father thinks."

"Well, you know what he's like, Pierre."

"I have had enough! I have been forced to enter a career in which I have no interest."

"But what will you do?"

"I don't know, Marie. I seriously don't know. It's time to break with these ridiculous traditions."

"0h, Pierre, I do hope you sort something out."

"Don't worry! At least we can see more of each other now. Why should I follow in their footsteps, like all the boring old fools I meet in the salons? Marie, we need ideals ... the world needs ideals. I need a goal, a dream to follow. This dream of Dr Brooke is a symbol of peace which could end all wars. I would rather follow this dream than fight."

"But, Pierre, be careful."

"I do love you, Marie, you know that," Pierre said, kissing her softly and embracing her.

***

Marie was not surprised at his decision. She had been supportive of him all along. In a way, he was emotionally dependent on her. They had corresponded by letter regularly while he was at St. Cyr. His loneliest hours were spent writing to her. She knew he was in love with her. He felt the same, except he could never express it. His aristocratic birth and upbringing had taught him a certain restraint. Marie was more flamboyant. At times she would kiss him spontaneously at the opera, and even in one of the many Parisian restaurants they frequented.

Pierre had been pre-occupied by his feelings for Marie for many months. He read Plato's book on love and desire. It helped him focus his emotions more finely. Plato's book 'The Phaedrus' explored the definitions of love, and the lover's search for perfection. Pierre copied Phaedrus's text into his diary:

Let us establish by mutual consent a definition of love that will explain its nature and its powers; and then with this to look back upon and refer to, let us proceed to consider, whether it is profitable or injurious in its results. Now that love is a kind of desire is clear to everyone, and equally clear on the other hand, that without being in love we desire beautiful objects. How then are we to see the lover? We should further observe that in every one of us there are two ruling and directing principles, whose guidance we follow wherever they may lead; the one being an innate desire for pleasure: the other an acquired judgment which aspires after excellence. When these two principles at one time maintain harmony we experience the emotion of love.

***

For Pierre love was a condition of the soul. Marie was his ideal, his desire; he had found perfection and harmony in her love.

They understood each other. That was the important thing. Marie had a difficult father too, who had engaged her in endless travel around Europe, following him on diplomatic missions. Now, since she had come of age, she refused to follow him.

The house where they had once lived in Alsace Lorraine was close to the German border. It was now boarded up and the servants had been dismissed. Her father had given her an annual allowance. Now she rented an apartment just off the Champs Elysees.

She was relieved that she no longer lived in Alsace. She, too, had childhood memories of German troops attacking the chateau during the Prussian War, burning the house down and killing many of the servants. It was an event she recalled vividly, even though she was only a small child at the time. She remembered seeing the giant chandeliers crashing to the marble floor in the main hallway, and flames destroying her father's paintings, including his favorite painting of the Pope painted by Pierre's father.

Her new life in Paris was filled with fun and pleasure. On many occasions they would meet at the Cafe Flore and drink coffee and discuss their plans for their future. Pierre would always enquire as to the contents of her last lecture at the Sorbonne, where she studied philosophy. It was here that they would spend their afternoons. Pierre respected her intelligence, unlike some of her suitors who treated her as a pretty object. Women in this society were supposed to be seen and not heard.

It was a world where it was accepted that every aristocrat had at least one mistress in some quarter of Paris. Pierre disliked this side of Parisian life, with its rampant prostitution. All across Paris hundreds of women carried out this profession in private bordellos, which served everyone from the baker to the king. It was said that some of Paris's finest bordellos catered for the royals of Europe, and their interior decoration would put the palace of Versailles to shame. It seemed that the whole of Parisian society was obsessed, in one way or another, with its search for pleasure. The aristocracy was diseased. The dreaded syphilis had spread like wildfire among the educated classes. Even a married woman was not safe from her husband's indiscretions.

Pierre did not feel that he was moralizing about the way in which colleagues chose to lead their lives. He felt that there ought to he another way of life. It should have a purpose, whereby something of value could be achieved. The moral and spiritual core of the French nation was rotten. Unless things changed drastically, it could collapse forever. It had happened to greater civilizations before. It seemed to Pierre that if one looked at Parisian society, it was now emulating the last days of the Roman Empire.

Paris had a great and noble past. Men had once fought for nobler ideals. This modern decadence should not destroy the true French spirit.

Paris had nurtured many writers, musicians and painters, like Dore, Ingres, Corot, Moliere, Delacroix, Balzac, Louis David, Bizet, Rousseau, Voltaire, Pascal, Racine, Offenbach, Berlioz, Dumas, Utrillo, Manet, Morisot, Debussy, Descartes, Maupassant and Baudelaire. Pierre was becoming more aware of this great intellectual tradition. Paris loved its geniuses.

When Victor Hugo died in 1885, all of France threw itself into an intense mourning. The coffin draped in black was laid in state under the Are de Triomphe. Two million Parisians followed this coffin to its final resting place in the Pantheon, paying tribute to a genius of France.

***

Some days after Pierre's return from England, he talked to his mother in the drawing room. He had not seen her for some time, as the Baroness often took trips to Vienna to see the new works of the Vienna Secessionists. She was a great lover of the architecture of Olbrich, and was obsessed by the beauty of Gustav Klimt's paintings. His father was nowhere to be seen and his brothers and sisters were at college. Pierre's mother greeted him with much warmth, kissed him on both cheeks, and they sat down to afternoon tea together.
"Where is Papa?" asked Pierre, curious about his whereabouts.

"He's gone to Rome. He has been commissioned by the Academy to paint the Pope again. He won't be back for some days. Papa is still very angry with you. I have tried to calm him down, but at times it is very difficult. Please forgive your father for being angry, but he has his reasons.

"What reasons?"

"You must understand, Pierre, he wants to see you have a career."

"Marie, Albert and Paul have careers, but that doesn't mean I have to follow in their footsteps."

"Yes, Pierre, I agree. This is where I disagree with your father ... He is obsessed by history ... our family history ... the duty to the throne of France and the Pope.... He believes you should follow this tradition, as did your ancestors. I must warn you, Pierre, he will disown you; you will not receive your inheritance. He will cast you aside as he did your great-uncle."

The words echoed around the room. Only the evening light streaming through the great windows gave Pierre some solace. The echo of his mother's words disappeared as quickly as they had been spoken.

***

OSCAR WILDE, WHO VISITED OLYMPIA,
AND THE ZAPPIAN OLYMPIC GAMES IN 1875.

CHAPTER SEVEN

PARIS 1894

So I too pass flowing nectar,
The Muses' gift, sweet fruit of the heart,
To men who win prizes,
And make them glad,
To winners at Olympia and Pytho. Happy is he
Who is held in good report.
Beauty, who gives strength to life,
Turns her eyes now on this man.

OLYMPIAN VII

The First Olympic Congress organised by Pierre was held in the Aux Maxima at the Sorbonne university Paris. The Mural above was painted puvis de chauvennes

PARIS 1894

As the weeks passed, Pierre prepared the plans for his project. He began to write to the newspapers about reviving the Games. His room began to fill with pamphlets, letters, correspondence to government ministers and people of influence across France. He appealed to their sense of duty, their love of France and of classical Greece. Letters were written bearing the insignia of de Coubertin. Daily he could be seen in the library of the Sorbonne, sitting under a table lamp, poring over ancient documents, reading everything he could find on the subject.

Pierre wrote in one of his letters: "Let us export our oarsmen, our runners, our fencers into other lands. That is the true free trade of the future and the day it is introduced into Europe the cause of peace will have received a new and strong ally ... I now propose ... the splendid and beneficent task of reviving the Olympic Games."

For weeks he had requested a meeting with the Minister for the Interior in the French government, a certain Monsieur Blont, but was rebuffed by his secretary several times. He persisted. Eventually a letter arrived from the Elysee Palace, giving him an audience with this highly placed bureaucrat.

He arrived there by carriage. He made his way through the vaulted corridors filled with Louis XIV furniture. Surely the government would listen to his plans? He was convinced that he would receive a favorable reaction.

***

In a Baroque room with an enormous vaulted ceiling he was greeted by Monsieur Blont and ushered to a chair.

"You must be Pierre ... what was it ...?"

"De Coubertin," replied Pierre.

"Yes, yes, that's right, take a seat ... I received your letter," said the minister, easing himself into the chair behind his desk, which was covered in papers, vases and a model of the Eiffel Tower.

"Yes, yes, where were we ... I can't seem to find your letter ... I'm so busy."

"Don't worry, sir, I have a copy."

"Marvelous ... would you like some?" said the minister, pointing to a tray of drinks on the cabinet.

"No, thank you, sir," replied Pierre nervously.

"Oh, I always have Russian vodka at midday," said Monsieur Blont, pouring himself a drink." Now, this letter ... you want to revive the Olympic Games ... you want support... money from the government."

"Yes, that's correct."

"Mmm... it's an interesting idea... but it's impossible... it simply won't work," said Monsieur Blont, gulping his vodka down.

"But why not?" asked Pierre.

"Look, for example, we have this chap coming in here with this model... he calls it the Eiffel Tower, after himself, of course. It's the ugliest looking building I've ever seen. This is a beautiful city built by Hausmann, we don't need this horrible steel tower slap in the middle of Paris. Every day I get these crackpots in with these new ideas. Now you want to revive the Olympics, a pagan festival in a Catholic country. It simply will not work."

"But the Games were about peace, about the finest achievements of men," said Pierre anxiously.

"Peace, love, ideals ... all very fine, Pierre, but they would be outraged by such an event, they're already screaming down my throat about this damn tower. What is your profession, my boy?"

"Well, I used to be a cadet."

"Well, my advice to you is to continue your career... forget this madness... it is too big a project for any one man. I'm sorry, but I cannot give your plans the seal of approval. To my mind, it's just another crackpot idea."

"How was this city built?" Pierre replied, standing up. "Only by men of vision... you sir, belong to a dying generation of old fools who support nothing of value and

destroy every idea before it can succeed. In my view, the Eiffel Tower is a masterpiece of design... and one day it will be built... and you will look back and realize what a stupid fool you were. Good day, Sir."

***

Pierre's meeting with M. Blont filled him with despair. He had always thought that those in a position of influence would have the sensitivity to understand new ideas, that their exalted position would naturally give them an exalted morality. He was beginning to learn of his own naivety. How closeted he had been in his grand old aristocratic world, where his social position had protected him! He would have to learn the game of politics, of how to manipulate the bureaucratic machine, if he was to achieve his ambition.

He had a new plan to set up a society for the revival of the ancient games. He would invite kings, princes and notable bureaucrats to sit on a committee. This would give it weight. It would not just be Pierre de Coubertin standing alone.

***

Marie visited him late one evening. She found Pierre unshaven, sitting at his desk. He looked like he had not slept for days. The endless correspondence was beginning to take its toll. He had continued to send countless letters, to the government ministers, kings, queens, princes and men of prestige.

Marie ran her hands through his hair and beckoned him to sit with her. She could see clearly the dark shadows under his eyes, bloodshot, with his eyelids drooping as if they wanted to sleep forever. He had the expression of a man possessed.

"You have to stop and rest, Pierre. It will do you good."

"I'm feeling depressed."

"Oh, Pierre, you poor thing. What are you going to do?"

"I have made my decision," said Pierre firmly." This idea about the Games is a great one … but how are you going to do it?" said Marie."

"Don't worry, Marie, I'll find a way."

"It's such an ambitious project. What you need is contacts, men of position to lend support. But Pierre, all this needs money.

Where will you get it from?"

"Don't worry, Marie, money is not a problem."

"Pierre, you really shouldn't cast your money away on such a risky project. You should think it through more carefully first this idea of yours, Pierre Are you really serious?"

"Of course I'm serious."

"But why .... why these Games? Why are they so important?" Because it is such a great ideal? You don't care, do you? You're like all the rest." Look, Pierre, you come from a good family. You have a good education. Now you are off pursuing this wild ambition."

Pierre did not reply. He lay back on the couch exhausted, closing his eyes. Marie wiped the beads of sweat from his brow. How long would he pursue this madness, she thought? She regretted that he had made this trip to England. If only Doctor Brooke had not given him this sacred cup! Marie sat with him for some time until Pierre was fast asleep. Then she sneaked away quietly, whispering some words of advice to the maid on the way out.

Marie had questioned him as to the value of continuing. But he could give her no reply. The issue of money spent was raised; Pierre could see that she was apprehensive. In England there had been a complete conversion at Dr. Brooke's house. Marie had tried to understand the driving force behind all his restless activity. Anchored at the very core of his life now was the paradox between his duty to his family and this great Olympic ambition.

Marie tried to understand Pierre's thoughts. The more they argued about Pierre's idea, the closer they felt. Even in the face of misunderstanding, the bonds of affection and simple unquestioning love seemed to increase. After all, she loved him. Even if she appeared apprehensive, it was only to try to protect him.

***

It was some days later that a letter arrived with the American flag printed on an envelope. He was surprised to learn that it was from a certain Professor Sloane, professor of history at Princeton University. Sloane had heard of Pierre's project from a recent article in 'Le Figaro.' He was in Paris researching a book on the 'French War and the Revolution'. He had studied at Leipzig University and served as private secretary to George Bancroft, the American envoy to Berlin.

Sloane was familiar with the history of the Olympics and classical philosophy. He was excited by Pierre's idea so much that he wanted him to join him at the American Embassy for dinner. Pierre was delighted that for the first time in many weary months someone wanted to listen to him, someone who had grasped the idea enthusiastically.

***

When Pierre and Marie arrived at the American Embassy, Professor Sloane of Princeton cast a great shadow across their path. He was a powerfully built figure with an enormous head, and a mane of flaxen hair swept back. He looked quite like Apollo. He had that engaging way of a man born with confidence. Pierre's new American friend was full of life. Sloane was an historian and a conversationalist, and an enormously generous human being with an expansive, vibrant nature. He greeted Marie and Pierre.

"Let me introduce you to Marie Rothan," said Pierre. "My dear

... you have a face like an angel!"

"Thank you, Monsieur Sloane," replied Marie." Come into my chambers," said Sloane, waving his hand.

They entered a large office with baroque furniture where Sloane served them drinks.

"Thank you for the invitation ... it is kind of you," said Pierre.

"Don't mention it, my boy. I was so impressed by your idea. I had to meet you," said Sloane, pulling heavily on his cigar.

"Pierre is full of wonderful ideas," said Marie, somewhat wistfully.

"Yes, but this idea of reviving the Olympics is a unique one. In fact, it's one of the most original ideas I've heard since I've arrived in Paris," said Sloane enthusiastically.

"Well, in America we are concerned with the future; we will listen to any man, wherever he's from. We are not obsessed by class or position like the British and the French. The games will be a wonderful way of creating a new internationalism, where each man will seek a new kind of perfection."

"Exactly. It will help destroy all this nationalism ... racism and create a new international community," agreed Pierre.

"I am glad that you have arrived on time. I have a little surprise for you. A very influential man will be arriving for the banquet."

"Who is he ?" asked Marie, excitedly.

"The President of America," said Sloane, pointing his finger at

Pierre;" and we're going to talk him into this great idea of yours," he added, lighting a cigar and getting up from his chair.

"It's such a great idea. You have got to try, Pierre! If you don't, you won't succeed ... you're a romantic, Pierre."

"... And what are you, Marie?" asked Pierre, smiling again.

"Your great love," said Marie, kissing him.

"Pierre, I can only admire your love of the Olympic idea", Sloane said," but you must be cautious. If you want it to have a meaning as a great and powerful symbol, then you must enlist support from every possible country. You are thirty now, you will see that many people who say that they will support you may not do anything for you. You will finally have to push it through yourself. It is a question of gaining support from patrons, both large and small. I believe that President Carnot admires your work very much, enlist his support. If the President of France is behind you all of France will be behind you. Pierre, I am almost three times your age, but please be assured that I deeply appreciate meeting a young idealist with an extraordinary dream."

***

The dining room had been laid with the finest cutlery and golden plates decorated with the insignia of the Embassy. The white table tops glowed with the light from the candelabra. It was a special occasion for everyone. President Cleveland had not visited France before. Sloane had sent him this invitation and was anxious to meet him. It was said he had an encyclopedic knowledge and could liven up any conversation.

***

After eight o'clock the guests arrived. They took their chairs while servants hurried with food and wine to the great long table. The master of ceremonies, dressed in a red uniform, entered and approached the table and he made three short taps with his little wooden hammer and announced the distinguished guest.

"Ladies and gentlemen, President Cleveland of America."

Pierre and Marie observed the imposing figure of the President enter with his wife, followed by an entourage of diplomats and servants. Sloane approached him with a great beaming smile and shook his hand, then gestured to Pierre and Marie and introduced them both.

"It's a pleasure to meet you... come and sit with me. Professor Sloane has written to me about your great idea," said the President, shaking their hands and introducing his wife. Then the President joined them at the banqueting table.

"What interests me about your idea is that the Greeks have had so much influence on the western world. Even the idea of a United States was a Greek one," said the President, sipping some wine.

"My idea, Mr President," replied Pierre," is for an international event with all the countries of the world united in the spirit of an ancient symbol - the sacred flame of peace ignited by the sun at Olympia."

"It's a great symbol, and symbols are very powerful. What you need to do, Pierre, is to create an Olympic Congress where delegates from all the different countries can attend. They can vote on a revival. It can also be a place where money can be raised," said the President, as if starting a new election campaign.

"Why not hold the games in America?" said Sloane enthusiastically.

"That's a good idea, but Athens is where it should be held first.

Use the symbols, Pierre, and use them wisely. I also think it's a good idea to set up a committee where men of power and position can be members. You see, Pierre, when you start recreating history, you must guide it towards a greater goal. Look at Professor Sloane, he can tell you about history. He has written a book about Napoleon and another one on the history of America," replied the President, lifting his glass.

"But how are we going to get a Congress together?" questioned Pierre.
"Yes, you need a committee inviting Kings, Queens and men of position to join. This will create support... but first get a Chairman... a man of position. Now let me see," said Sloane looking down the long table to an old bearded man wearing round glasses." Yes, Jules Simon, former Prime Minister of France."

"An excellent idea, I would think."

Sloane motioned to one of the footmen and whispered in his ear. An invitation was extended to Simon to join them in the discussion. The former Prime Minister took a seat beside them.

"Yes, I have heard of Pierre's idea - it's a wonderful one - but getting a project off the ground in France is difficult, at the best of times."

"Would you consider becoming Chairman of a new Olympic Committee?" asked Pierre.

"Well I am Chairman of many committees already; one more won't make much difference."

"Excellent," replied Pierre.

"Let's call it the Jules Simon Committee."

"Agreed."

"But we should organize a meeting immediately, together with a banquet. We need to send out invitations. Let us entertain our guests."

"A clever strategy," replied Pierre.

"If I have the time, I would very much like to visit Troy," said Simon." When I was younger I wanted to visit St. Petersburg. To think that one can find Parisian buildings and classical temples in Russia!"

***

Simon had striking grey hair and, although burly, was swift in movement, as if impatient that things were not going more quickly. There was no hurry as he spoke; however, his voice was mellow and easy. It was almost as if he was talking to himself and allowing one to overhear. It was neither oratory nor preaching. He was so skilled as a rhetorician that he allowed you to think along with him, to arrive at the same conclusion without any sense of having been conducted there. He soothed the listener with his voice and sometimes, for a moment, one was lulled by the lovely cadences, the easy, full sound, so like listening to the cello.

It was impossible to think that the same man, now sitting back in an easy chair, had given some of the most impassioned speeches, and that audiences were moved to tears when he spoke about his first and deepest love, France. Behind the extraordinary composure, there appeared a passionate mind capable of admiring Voltaire and Byron's poetry.

If Charles de Coubertin had been displeased by Pierre's refusal to follow in the family tradition and enter the army, he would have been absolutely astonished to hear that Pierre had enlisted the help of Jules Simon. Simon was among France's immortals - a member of the French Academy - and an orator of the highest talents.

It had not been a foregone conclusion that Simon would help. Pierre and he came from very different worlds, but they met at the intersection of an ideal. Simon had the absolute kindness of a man of power, but it was a kindness which could refuse as well as grant requests. Jules Simon agreed to accept a seat on the committee as president until the direction of the Olympic Sports Union became more secure.

"Have you had any response from the government yet?" asked Simon.

"Not yet they're too busy with the great Exposition. I am beginning to spend money on these banquets. Marie is very worried about this. But who will pay for it if I don't?" You have to work fast, Pierre. If you do have a congress, make it an impressive one make sure they don't forget you! You can hold it at the Sorbonne," said Jules excitedly." The Sorbonne!" replied Pierre." Yes, I know the President. I will talk to someone tomorrow. You need a great hall at the Sorbonne; it's a very impressive one. Don't worry, Pierre, I'll send a letter to President Carnot requesting his support. You must become master of your own destiny. If you really want to revive the Games, you must fight all the way." The Congress should have hundreds of supporters, screaming for Olympism, and demanding to relight the flame." Do you know, Pierre, there was a plan to revive the Games in America", said Sloane." I have a record of it in my papers. It is a copy of a document sent to President Josiah Willard of Harvard written 1788. It mentions an eventual rebirth of the Olympic Games in America".

At that moment Marie held Pierre's hand. She looked radiant in her long velvet evening dress. Her pearl earrings shone in the light. Her red lips were in sharp contrast to her pale complexion.

A beautiful pearl necklace was draped around her neck. Then she smiled at him like she never had before.

***

The meeting with the President and the former Prime Minister had pleased Pierre. Here was the American President talking enthusiastically about his project. An Olympic Congress and a revival in Athens were excellent ideas. He was beginning to understand the relationship between politics and symbolism. The symbols gave it a meaning all of its own. America had founded its great union, symbolized in the statue of liberty holding up the flame and in the flag of stars and stripes. Its constitution echoed in the declaration of independence the granting of equality to all men. If Pierre was to revive the ancient Games he would have to gather his own symbols together. He also would have to write his own declarations, set out in an Olympic Charter.

Sloane pointed out during the course of the meeting that it was the French who had made this declaration of freedom and equality during the Revolution. The Americans had followed the French ideal. This had brought American Union one step further.

When would Europe become united? When would this great Greek ideal become a reality? Pierre would try to forge these links. For the era it was an extraordinary ambition. The idea of creating games for all nations to compete in seemed almost impossible. How would Pierre achieve it?

Pierre spent several weeks talking with Sloane about his plans. The professor had promised that he would try to rally support in America. He would be only too willing to attend an Olympic Congress, if Pierre could organize one in France. If not, Princeton might be an alternative location. America would support the project, but Pierre felt that the President's advice should be taken seriously. A revival in the place of origin would be a fitting symbol. Marie, for the first time, was beginning to realize Pierre's conviction. They had only been back in Paris a few months when Pierre set the wheels in motion.

His first plan had been to set up this committee under the chairmanship of Jules Simon. He was anxious to throw a banquet immediately. He made out the invitations, embossed with the statue of Nike, goddess of Victory.

***

Pierre needed to reflect as he walked through the streets of Paris. Paris by night was a city where whores lingered in doorways, musicians played and revelers of all sorts sung drunken songs. He walked until dawn approached and the air was filled with mist. At that hour one could see the light of the flickering street lamps, fusing with the twilight. Figures that crossed his path always seemed to move in the half light, like ghosts in the night. Here was a side of Paris that many respectable Parisians rarely saw. He could smell the opium in the air. Sometimes he could see through thewindows where on velvet Moroccan pillows men and women lay motionless, gazing towards the ceiling in smoke-filled rooms.

***

In recent days Pierre had begun to neglect Marie. It was not that he no longer loved her, but his energy seemed to be devoted now to one single goal. When Pierre had returned from one of his midnight walks, his servant announced the arrival of a young lady. Marie was visibly upset when she entered the room. She did not look into his eyes and kiss him as she always did. She sat opposite him without removing her hat, in her long velvet winter coat.

"Why have you not contacted me?" she said in a whisper.

"Forgive me, Marie, but I have been quite busy."

"Yes, I can see," said Marie looking at a pile of letters on the floor." But what about our relationship? Have you still any feelings for me?"

"Of course I have."

"Well, why don't you show them instead of burying yourself amongst all these papers?"

"I'm sorry, Marie. There's a banquet to be held at the Sorbonne at the end of the month. You will come, won't you?"

"I'm not sure, Pierre. I've been thinking a lot about us recently and our relationship - I'm concerned about you spending so much time and money on this project. It seems you have less and less time for me. I am concerned that you will squander your inheritance on this project. My father is of the opinion that you are not a suitable suitor for me. He says you have a gambling nature. You've been throwing parties and banquets, and spending your money. He thinks you've gone mad, that you're a reckless adventurer, that you will just marry me on a whim." Marie,

I need your support. I would never do anything to destroy what we have together."

"Yes, but Pierre, it has happened to many young girls in Paris. They have married some adventurer, and before they know it they are on the streets. The lives of these girls have just fallen apart. My father is worried about my honor and our family name."

"I promise you, I promise you I will succeed. The Olympic Congress will he a success. I'll make your father proud of me," said Pierre, holding her hand.

"I love you, Marie. You know that!"

Just as Pierre's declaration of love ended, a servant entered and informed him that a young man named Michael Breal had arrived to see him. They would have to cut short this romantic encounter.

***

This young man was ushered into the hallway by the servant. In appearance he was imposing. His lean figure and fair hair was set off to perfection by his long black coat and cravat. His steely blue eyes seemed to light up as he approached them.

"Monsieur Michael Breal," announced the servant.

"Michael, I am pleased to see you. May I introduce you to Marie Rothan?" said Pierre.

"Delighted to meet you, Monsieur," said Marie, shaking his hand." Would you like some tea?"

"Yes, indeed," said Michael, taking a porcelain cup.

"Michael is a student at the Sorbonne," explained Pierre to Marie." I received your letter the other day, Michael... you're studying the classics."

"Yes, indeed. I was fascinated by your article in the paper the other day about the Olympic revival."

"Well, tell me, what can I do for you?" said Pierre.

"I want to propose a race, a great race for the congress. The marathon. A perfect symbol of victory over war," replied Michael.

"I don't understand," said Pierre.

"Marathon was where the Greeks defeated the Persians... after the battle, the Greek, Pheippides, ran all the way to Athens to tell the good news, a distance of twenty six miles", replied Michael.

"Twenty six miles", said Pierre." I didn't know anyone could run so far."

"Well, Pheippides did drop dead, but I'm sure it can be done," said Michael.

"Yes," said Pierre thoughtfully.

"I want to show you something, something very sacred." Then Pierre unwrapped the sacred cup and placed it on the table." This was the cup that held the oil that lit the Olympic flame ... fifteen hundred years ago ... I'd like the winner of the Marathon to have it."

"Oh, Pierre, it's beautiful," said Michael." Yes, this cup is to be passed on."

Michael asked," Will you propose this at the congress?" Certainly," replied Pierre.

"You ought to start planning our strategy now," said Michael." Yes, I agree," said Pierre.

"You must seize the opportunity. You won't get another," said Michael.

"Yes, I realize that. The marathon is a great idea, but let's do it properly. Let's do it in Greece, the race from Marathon to Athens, the Games brought back to life, where they started," said Pierre.
"Wonderful," said Marie." That's brilliant! Athens! But when?" asked Michael.

"Let's do it immediately, next year, Athens 1896," said Pierre." Am I to understand the Congress is going ahead?"

"That is correct."

"What is your strategy? Are you going to get approval for the Athens Games?"

"Well, I'm going to try ... Prince Constantine of Greece is coming."

"I am excited by your idea. This great revival, if you can make it possible."

***

Pierre did not see Marie for some weeks after this encounter.

Meanwhile the gossip raged in Paris. Why, they wondered, did Pierre engage in such a pointless quest? In his innermost thoughts Pierre now had his own doubts. Could international co-operation ever work in practice?

He received a letter from Berlin stating that the Germans would not take part in the Olympic Congress due to the fact that the French were involved. Pierre was informed that the Germans had taken offence at remarks he was supposed to have made. 'But Pierre denied that he had made these comments. It was too late; the National-Zeitung had printed them throughout Germany. Frantically, Pierre sent out letters denying the 'insane' allegations. He contacted General Schwartzkoppen at the German embassy in Paris. From the beginning he was sympathetic. He promised that he would try to persuade his colleagues to come. It was many weeks later before he was informed that the Germans had agreed to come unofficially.

Pierre felt alone during this time. He thought of the consequences of Marie's father's rejection. He would have to wait. The nights for him seemed longer, and sometimes he would sit up late and write endless letters to delegates. He was becoming more and more exhausted with the administration and endless correspondence.

***

It was Michael Breal who introduced Pierre and Marie some days later to the sculptor of the Statue of Liberty, Frederic Auguste Bartholdi. Bartholdi had built the giant statue at the entrance of New York Harbor. This statue of a woman in robes holding up a giant torch - a sacred flame illuminating the world had been named 'The Statue of Liberty.' It was said that Bartholdi was so in love with his wife that he had copied her beautiful features as the statute's face.

It was made possible with the collaboration of several individuals: Edouard-Rene Lefebvre de Laboulaye, whose concept it was; Alexandre Gustave Eiffel, the engineer, who designed the supporting framework; Richard Morris Hunt, the architect, who designed the pedestal; General Charles P. Stone, the Civil War veteran, who supervised the construction; and Joseph Pulitzer whose newspaper campaign for funds for the statue aroused the generosity of thousands of people in France and the United States.,

Bartoldi told Pierre that it was at Versailles the idea had been put forward at a dinner party given by the host Edouard de Laboulaye, the author of a three-volume Histoire des Etats-Unis. It was at this party that Laboulaye discussed his idea of building for America a monument to the ideal of Liberty. Present that evening was the thirty-one year-old sculptor from Alsace, Frederic Auguste Bartholdi, whose one ambition in life was to build the greatest statues the world had seen.

Ever since his first visit to Egypt, in 1856, when he had admired the Sphinx at Cairo, Bartholdi had had plans to create a monumental work. His other project was to build a lighthouse in the form of a massive robed female figure to be erected at the entrance of the Suez Canal. Its title would be 'Egypt Carrying the Light to Asia'. Like liberty enlightening the world, the design was of an idealized female figure on a giant scale holding a torch, symbolizing peace and liberty.

Since at least the third century B.C., when the Romans built a temple to the Goddess of Liberty, it had been traditional to use the figure of a robed woman to symbolize certain civic and religious virtues. Pierre recalled Eugene Dalacroix's dramatic painting of Liberty - bayonet in one hand, tricolor in the other advancing over the bodies of her fallen comrades.

The image of liberty, carrying the flame, echoed for Pierre the statue of Athena carrying the flame of peace. The flame now adopted by the Americans would become his Olympic symbol too. Inscribed on a plaque on the plinth of the statue were the words of Emma Lazarus, taken from her book 'The New Colossus.'

Not like the brazen giant of Greek fame,
With conquering limbs astride from land to land;
Here at our sea-washed, sunset gates shall stand
A mighty woman with a torch, whose flame
Is the imprisoned lightning, and her name
Mother of Exiles. From her beacon-hand
Glows world-wide welcome; her mild eyes command
The air-bridged harbor that twin cities frame.
"Keep, ancient lands, your storied pomp!" cries she
With silent lips." Give me your tired, your poor,
Your huddled masses yearning to breathe free,
The wretched refuse of your teeming shore.
Send these, the homeless, tempest-tots to me,
I lift my lamp beside the golden door."

***

JOHN PENTLAND MAHAFFY,
HEAD OF CLASSICS TRINITY COLLEGE,
WHO ATTENDED THE ZAPPIAN GAMES
WITH OSCAR WILDE IN 1875.

CHAPTER EIGHT

VERSAILLES 1889

*To each man come different goods, and many
Are the paths of success
When the Gods give help.*

OLYMPIANAN VII

A Ball in the Gardens at Versailles.

Pierre planned now for an Olympian Ball where each guest would dress up as an Olympic God. Once again he set about sending out invitations. This time he had special ones printed with a painting of Louis XIV as Apollo and his family as Olympian Gods. The finest vineyards supplied the wines and champagnes. An Italian orchestra was engaged to play some of the best classical melodies. Parisian society waited with bated breath to receive Pierre's invitation.

Late one afternoon he received a letter from Dr. Brooke. He expressed how much he would like to see Pierre again. He was unable to travel now, because he had been ill for some time and was confined to bed. He said he had thought often about Pierre and read of his progress. It was all that preoccupied him. He no longer practiced as a doctor. His letter was almost hallucinatory, the words of a dying man. Dr. Brooke wrote that in the mornings he was woken early by the light streaming through his small window. He would observe a small bust of Athena that seemed to come to life in the shimmering light. He imagined her talking to him of the Gods of Olympia, and reminding him of his life's work.

Pierre replied immediately, and told him of the American President's visit. For the first time he admitted to Brooke that the project had given him a great purpose in life. He thanked him for his inspiration and wished him well. The doctor suggested that he write to Constantine of Greece on Pierre's behalf. He proposed that Pierre should write to Constantine and the King of Greece also. He further suggested that a Mr. Vikelas be appointed President of the Paris Congress. Vikelas was a Greek academic who had spent most of his life in France. He was deeply involved in Greek politics and literature.

It was Prince Constantine's view that Vikelas should be appointed President of the Committee. This would help bring the games to Athens. Dr. Brooke's plan was that before the Congress should take place a strategy should be worked out. De Coubertin, Vikelas and Constantine would together revive the Athens games. A week later Pierre was to receive confirmation of the Hellenic plan in a confidential document issued by Prince Constantine.

Pierre had planned the great Paris Congress of June 1894. One of the main items on the agenda concerned amateurism. No athlete could take part in the games for money or personal gain. This was another concept which was not found in the original Olympic Games and developed by Pierre. But Pierre's main aim for this Congress was a grand plan for Athens 1896.

***

Pierre stood on the steps of Versailles as the evening light was fading. Torches blazed around him, all along the facade. As he looked down the avenue he could see a trail of carriages making their way towards the palace. Pierre was dressed as Ulysses, King of Ithaca, and Marie as the Goddess of Love. She crept up behind him and kissed him on the cheek.

"All of Paris will be here tonight ... Olympic fever is just beginning," said Pierre.

"Has the orchestra arrived?"

As Marie spoke, strains of Bach could be heard on the terrace. Pierre admired Marie's head-dress of laurel leaves and her long flowing white dress.

They entered the magnificent ballroom once again. They watched as the guests arrived. It was a colorful sight of feathers, masks and all the gods and goddesses of Greek mythology come to life: Zeus, Poseidon, Hera... the list was endless. Everyone was unrecognizable in costume. People began to cavort and dance, while others sat at the banqueting tables eating and drinking.

Pierre turned to Marie and kissed her, then took a little velvet box from a leather pouch.

"What is it, Pierre?" said Marie, quite surprised.

"It's for you ... I bought it in Paris yesterday."

Pierre opened the box to reveal a ring encrusted in diamonds.

"It's the most beautiful ring I have ever seen!"

"Yes, Marie, it is especially for you... will you marry me?

"Oh, Pierre, I don't know what to say," replied Marie, quite emotional.

She hesitated for a moment, casting her eyes across the ballroom floor. Pierre waited nervously, as if the moment was an eternity. "Oh, of course I will," said Marie, kissing him," but you know it is only proper for me to follow tradition."

"What tradition?"

"I have to get my father's permission."

Pierre noticed the arrival of Jules Simon who hurried over waving a piece of paper. The Comte made his way over to him. "What is it, Jules?"

"I've just come from the Elysee," said Jules, quite out of breath.

He handed a letter to Pierre, who read it quickly and then beamed a huge smile.

"The President has agreed to help finance the Olympic Congress. We've got the Sorbonne too."

"Marvellous, Pierre. It's wonderful!" said Marie, elated at the news."You've done it !"

"What would I have done without you both?" replied Pierre, shaking Jules hand."We also have an extended invitation to the Paris Exposition."

Pierre danced the night away with Marie. He was in love and his dream was beginning to take shape. He had now truly entered the world of Olympism and he would become its champion. The Gods that had lain dormant for thousands of years were about to come to life.

***

Pierre's elation was short lived. On returning home he learned of his father's arrival from the country. His mother informed him that his presence was requested at breakfast.

"So I have read the morning papers," said his father reading aloud."Pierre de Coubertin, son of Baron Charles, recently announced his intention to revive the Olympic Games. What is the meaning of this? You might at least have thought of your family before dragging our name through the mud like this... and for what? This is madness."

"I did not think you would disapprove," responded Pierre.

"Well, first you drop out of the Academy, then you run off to

England to see that madman, the Comte de Paris... now this! Was it he who put this idea into your head?"

"No, father, not at all."

The Baron shuffled some papers in his drawer and then angrily waved them at Pierre.

"These arrived this morning. Bills from everywhere in Paris... banquets, crates of champagne, a printing bill for invitations, bills for cooks, waiters, orchestras and food... It comes to thousands of francs. Are you out of your mind? This has to stop immediately. I have instructed your trustees to cut off your funds," said Charles, leaving the room, where Pierre sat despondently looking out across the lawn.

***

Pierre was too distressed to talk to Marie about what had happened. His mind turned to the invitations, to the celebrations for Bastille day. Marie and Pierre arrived by carriage at Place de la Concorde and were greeted by the wonderful sight of the great steel tower created by Gustav Eiffel for the Exposition. Monsieur Blont had said it was madness, but Gustav Eiffel's project was now a reality. Pierre was encouraged by the sight of this new wonder gracefully sweeping into the sky above Paris.

Beneath the tower Pierre was greeted by Jules Simon. A brass band boomed across the plaza. Army cadets and members of the French government lined up in front of a red tape. All eyes fixed on President Carnot, who arrived in full military uniform. Then they watched fireworks exploding across Paris.

They took the lift to the top of the tower and gazed for the first time at the wondrous view. They felt like angels observing their beloved city. Paris glowed in the lights of the exploding fireworks. Beneath them thousands of people revelled in the streets, celebrating this new revolution of the spirit.

***

Pierre received a letter one morning from the King of Greece. He strongly suggested the appointment of Mr. Vikelas, the Greek gentleman of letters who lived in Paris, to the position as president of the congress and the proposed International Committee. He warned that Pierre would have to tread carefully in Greek politics. Vikelas would be his ally in his difficult plan.

Some days later he met with Vikelas, a distinguished man who was deeply surprised and flattered by the king's suggestion. Yet he accepted his new post gladly. If the king of Greece had summoned him, he, a loyal subject of Greece, would carry out the royal request.

***

Zeus, at Olympia. De Coubertin found the Olympic Rings beneath the statue of Zeus and painted them in five colours, creating the Olympic flag.

CHAPTER NINE

PARIS 1894

Go farther than others. No single training
Will look after all of us.
All skills are steep, but bring this prize
And boldly roar aloud
That by divine will this man has been born,
Strong of hand, lithe of limb,
With valour in his eyes,
And by his victory, Aias Ileus' son,
In your feast he has crowned our altar.

OLYMPIAN IX

Heinrich Schliemann
The German archeologist
who discovered Troy

The great day arrived, Saturday 16th June, 1894. The Olympic Congress was held in the Aula Maxima of the Sorbonne. A specially commissioned mural of the Sacred Heart was mounted on the back wall, painted by Puvis de Chavannes. There was a public performance of the"Delphic Hymn to Apollo", translated by Theódore Reinach. The composer, Gabriel Faure, wrote a choral to the ancient melody with harps and a great choir. Jeanne Remacle of the Opera sang the ode. This marvellous hymn had been discovered in the French School at Athens the previous year.

Pierre wrote of the effect these magical harmonies had on the audience:"The two thousand persons present listened in a religious silence to the divine melody risen from the dead to salute the Olympic renaissance across the darkness of the ages. The sacred harmony plunged the great audience into the ambience hoped for. A sort of subtle emotion flowed as the ancient eurythmy sounded across the distance of the ages. Hellenism thus infiltrated the vast enclosure. In these first hours, the Congress had come to a head. Henceforth I knew, consciously or not, that no one would vote against the restoration of the Olympic Games".

Pierre had received letters of support from their Majesties, the King of the Hellenes and the King of the Belgians. Also the Crown Prince of Sweden and His Imperial Highness the Grand Duke Vladimir, to whom he had offered the title of Honorary Members of the Congress. Baron de Courcil, Senator and former ambassador of France to Berlin, had agreed to accept the chairmanship. Delegates from England (Sir John Astley, President of the London Sports Club; Lord Dufferin, British Ambassador in Paris; and Charles Herbert from the Amateur Athletic Association), America, Sweden, Spain, Italy, Belgium and Russia were present. Professor Sloane of Princeton University, Mr Kemeny of Hungary, General de Boutowski of Russia, and

Major Balck of Sweden were in attendance. Prince Constantine of Greece had come also, lending Greece's support.

Pierre received a letter from Dr. Brooke. He apologised that he could not attend due to his age and poor health.

"I feel assured of the establishment of an international Olympian Association and the arrangement that such gatherings shall be held in rotation in or near the capitals of nations joining our movement. This has long been a cherished idea of mine insofar as making Greece the centre, but the plan of your congress embracing, as it does, all nations is a really superb one and deserving of the liberal support of all nations ... I wish I were younger and able to have the pleasure of attending your congress."

Inside the main hall, at the Olympic Congress, were seated the Chairman and the Committee, who faced a large audience. The Chairman addressed the audience, and a photographer under the hooded cape took a photograph.

The Chairman, Baron de Courcel, coughed and cleared his throat. He began,"Ladies and Gentlemen, welcome to the opening of the International Olympic Congress. We have with us today seventy nine delegates from thirteen different countries. All are supporting our campaign. We have had a great many messages of support from twenty one other countries. I now hand you over to Monsieur Jean Aicard, the poet and President of the Association of the Men of Letters."

Monsieur Aicard stood up and gazed around the room," I think there is little for me to say. I think Monsieur de Coubertin really embodies the Olympic ideal. We now see before us the fruits of his hard work. You will all wish to hear him. So then, may I call on him without more ado, a man that many of you know well, our president, Baron Pierre de Coubertin."

Jean Aicard took his seat. The audience broke into applause. Pierre addressed them." Never before have so many nations gathered in one place, with one common objective, of reviving the Olympic Games. I put it to you, ladies and gentlemen, that these Games should be held every four years. Every nation must be invited to participate. None should be excluded. I have here a telegram from his Royal Majesty, King George of Greece. He tenders to us his warmest thanks for proposing the revival of the Games.

"I would like to announce that my colleague, Monsieur Michael Breal has suggested a new Olympic event - the Marathon. It is to be run over twenty six miles. This was the same distance that the courier Pheidippides ran. He ran from Marathon to Athens to tell the Athenian people of their victory over the Persians. His dying words were:" Rejoice, we have conquered!" I propose that the race be run along the very route taken by Pheidippides. I propose that the winner be awarded a golden cup. This race will be run as a symbol of victory over war."

This was greeted with a standing ovation. Picrre raised his hand. The audience fell silent again.

"We shall relight the flame and recreate the Olympic Games, in Athens!"

With these words the audience leapt to their feet cheering. Pierre began again:" My friends, as you know, we had originally planned to hold the Games six years from now. Let me ask you something. Can we wait any longer? Can we wait to spread the Olympic ideal throughout the world? I know you want a better understanding between the nations. I want to put a new proposal before you. That we hold the Games in 1896! I would now like to introduce the Hymn to Apollo translated from the Greek by Professor Reinach. It is sung by Madame Remacle under the direction of Gabriel Faure. It is a hymn which can best be summed up in the immortal words of St. Catherine, 'All things are created by mystery and by love'".

The hymn began, its beautiful melody wafted across the audience. The audience broke into spontaneous applause. The delegates streamed onto the terrace.

***

In the courtyard, a runner bearing a torch passed beneath the archway. He ran up the flight of steps and set alight a flame in a large bowl. The crowd cheered and shouted"Athens! 1896!"

On the terrace that night Pierre and Marie stood watching the delegates flooding into the courtyard. They turned to face each other, laughing in delight. Vikelas introduced Pierre to Prince Constantine.

"You must come to Greece. You have my full support," said Constantine.

"It's a wonderful idea, but it may be difficult convincing the Greek government," said Vikelas.

"That is true ... Greece has little time and perhaps more to the point, few funds for such projects. But I will talk to my father ... he may have some influence. Vikelas, you must bring Monsieur de Coubertin to the palace," replied Prince Constantine.

" It would be an honour and a pleasure," replied Pierre.

"And who knows, the Gods may indeed look down upon us, said Constantine.

Pierre saw Sloane making his way down the corridor. It had been almost two years since he had last seen him. He still looked full of energy and enthusiasm. Sloane, he knew, would stir things up, and inject enthusiasm into the project. He greeted him warmly.

"Pierre, my boy, so good to see you," boomed Sloane, as tie shook hands with Pierre. "May I say what a privilege it is to be here tonight. That was the most inspirational speech. I can't wait to tell our boys back home. They'll love it. Anything you want me to do for you, just let me know. You want an American team? We'll be there," said Sloane enthusiastically.

"Thank you, that is most kind," said Pierre.

"Not at all. Tell me, Pierre. What is it that drives you on ? How 'have you come all this way?"

"A little faith, Professor Sloane," replied Pierre.

"Perhaps you are right. Frankly, I don't know. Some men climb mountains, some run races. But you've taken a fair bit of criticism in the past?"

"Naturally, it's the way with all new ideas, but today I think they listened," said Pierre.

"They sure did. People are moved by your sincerity, Pierre.""It just takes so long to move men's hearts," replied Pierre.

"But when you do, Pierre, it's wonderful," said Sloane, slapping him on the back.

"I don't think the Greeks will approve of me as President of the I.O.C. We have all the members of the committee now. The best plan is to make Vikelas the President. I think the Greeks would approve, and I will become secretary."

"But, Pierre, surely you should be President. After all, it's your idea."

"I know, Professor Sloane, but we must be realistic. Give the Greeks some glory and they may rise to the occasion."

***

The following day, in the conference room at the Sorbonne, a group of delegates gathered for the first meeting of the International Olympic Committee. They included Pierre de Coubertin, secretary of the I.O.C., Demetrios Vikelas, President of the I.O.C., General A. Boutowsky, Russia, Dr. Wilhelm Gebhardt, Germany, Jiri Guthjarkovsky, Bohemia, Franz Kemeny, Hungary, and General Viktor Balck, Sweden. Pierre addressed them.

"The congress has received unanimous support from the seventy nine delegates. Forty nine associations from twelve countries are present. They have been invited here today to establish the first International Olympic Committee. I propose that it should be independent, international and sovereign, a supreme body that would promote the physical and moral qualities which are the basis of sport. Secondly it would educate young people through sport in a spirit of better understanding, to help build a better and more peaceful world. Its aim is to spread the Olympic ideal, and bring together the athletes of the world in a great four yearly festival, beginning in Athens, 1896."

He woke early the following morning and wrote to Marie.

"I have become aware of the enormity of the task which I have undertaken in proclaiming the restoration of the Olympic games after an interruption of 1500 years. I can see all the hazards which will dog me on the way."

***

The first I.O.C meeting
Balck-Sweeden ,Boutovsky-Russia, Kemeny-Hungary,
Vikelas-Greece, Jarkowsky-Bohemia, De Coubertin-France,
Gebhardt-Germany

CHAPTER TEN

PARIS 1895

In return for reverence
Men's prayers are accomplished.
0 wooden place of Pisa by Alpheos,
Welcome this company and wearing of garlands.
His glory is great for ever.

OLYMPIAN VIII

Professor Sloane, Professor of Philosophy and History
Princeton University
Organiser of the American team.

Pierre's servant opened the curtains and a blaze of sunlight entered the room. He was informed that his father requested to see him in the library as soon as he awoke. Charles was to be found sitting at his great canvas of the Pope. He was silent for a moment. Then he turned and placed the paint brushes back on his small painting tray.

"I have been waiting for you, Pierre."

"Why?" questioned Pierre, a little puzzled.

"I was worried. How did the Congress go?"

'Oh, yes, the Congress. Couldn't have gone better. We're going to have the Olympics next year, in Athens."

"You've spent most of your inheritance already on this madness ... And what do you mean when you say the Games are going to be held next year?"

"Exactly that."

"And you've got the Greek government's agreement to this scheme, I take it?"

"Not exactly ... but Constantine, the Greek prince, has agreed to help me."

"Are you serious? Do you realise what you have done?""Yes, I have every one's support."

"Can't you see, you fool, you've set yourself up to be the laughing stock of Paris? Half the world was present at the Congress, the whole of Paris knows about it, and you haven't even got a commitment from the Greeks, yet."

***

Pierre retired to his room, upset by his father's comments. He realised that there was an element of truth in what he had said. It was true, there was no formal agreement with the Greeks. However, he had the support of the Congress. Now the hour had come for him to go to Greece and try and persuade the Greek government to accept the idea. A letter was despatched immediately to Athens requesting an audience with the Prime Minister, Tricoupis.

***

In England, the news of the Games for Athens travelled fast. The Comte de Paris read about the success of the Congress and related this news to Dr. Brooke . Sadly, only a faint smile could be found on Dr. Brooke's face. It seemed his prolonged illness had weakened him.

"It's very good of you to come, Monsieur, the doctor's been very poorly these last few days," whispered the housekeeper when the Comte arrived.

"Dr. Brooke, I have some good news for you. It's about Pierre," said the Comte.

"Pierre?" said Dr. Brooke meekly, with no expectancy in his voice.

"He's done it. Pierre has finally done it. The International Congress voted to hold the Games in Athens, next year," said the Comte.

Dr. Brooke was silent for a while. He sat looking at the statue of Athena on his desk.

"After all these years, I don't believe it. The Gods are with him ... Oh, Pierre, my boy, my boy," said Dr. Brooke in a whisper, gripping the Comte's hand and overcome by emotion.

***

That evening, Pierre and Marie were dining in a restaurant in Paris. They talked about all that had happened. They noticed a group of men talking nervously in the hallway. Suddenly, a deadly hush spread through the restaurant. A waiter appeared and made an announcement.

"Ladies and gentlemen, I must tell you that the President has been assassinated in Lyons."

***

Some days later, Marie called on Pierre. She found him in deep distress over the President's death. She consoled him and indeed encouraged him to continue his work on the games. She carressed his forehead and whispered quietly to him,

"Father was very impressed by the success of the congress. He's given me permission to marry you."

Pierre's face lit up in a smile, his face seemed to glow. He closed his eyes and kissed her sweetly.

***

MARCH 12, 1895

Weeks later at the church at Versailles their wedding ceremony took place. The vaulted dome covered in Baroque paintings was illuminated in the light of thousands of candles. A close group of

Pierre and Marie's friends gathered at the altar, including a number of pages and servants.

***

Marie wrote in her diary that night,

"My love for Pierre is now complete. My secret desire to be close to him and to love him has been granted. God is truly on our side. I can see he grows in confidence every day. I know now his passion for the Games belongs to the intensity of his love for me. He fulfills all my desires. I am frightened to tell him how much I love him and how much I desire him. His vision sometimes is beyond me. It is a panorama greater than our love for each other. I will support him to the end. I will never abandon him in his quest. My love must never fail. The flame belongs to our love."

***

They sat on the terrace at their hotel at Balbec and under a moonlit sky kissed each other passionately. It was then that Pierre proposed Marie go to Athens with him. She willingly consented.

On the day of departure Michael came to say good-bye to them. As the train sped down through France, Pierre and Marie discussed their plans.

"We've got to work out our strategy for Athens. Constantine's been trying to lobby the Prime Minister. He says we've got to appeal to Greek national pride," said Pierre.

"That's our problem. Constantine often wonders whether his government is really interested in such things as culture and history. Greece now is faced with sheer economic problems," replied Marie.

"I'm sure we can appeal to their heroic nature."

"Don't be so sure, or too optimistic. The Olympic Congress may mean nothing to the Greeks. They may think you're living in an ivory tower," said Marie cautiously.

***

The train travelled through the Loire valley and arrived at the harbour at Marseilles where Pierre and Marie boarded the steam ship, 'Ortegal'.

They observed with pleasure the turquoise water of the Mediterranean. Thin lines of white foam shimmered in the heat. From the deck of the boat Pierre could see the fish underwater. He observed moving clouds, little wisps along the gentle coast. After the calm of the early morning the first breezes started to ripple the surface of the crystalline sea. During the day, when stronger gusts came, one could see the wheeling of the gulls above the breaking foam.

In the evening the blue-grey surface was full of shallow waves, their white caps indicating the flow of the current. There was an extraordinary pink and orange light which illuminated the distant headland with a honey-yellow glow. The light of the day revealed everything.

They sailed past Sardinia. Pierre remembered that these were the same waters that Ulysses sailed on his wanderings from Troy. Pierre was now taking a journey not unlike Ulysses. Ulysses's homeland Ithaca appeared to the east. The Greek mainland was not too far away. The thin white line of sandy beaches could be seen shimmering in the heat. Dolphins and many-coloured fish swam in the sparkling, clear, blue waters. Pierre observed an ancient Greek temple on a hilltop, its golden edifice sculpted with scenes from a glorious past. Many great heroes had visited this mainland to fight for the Greek cause. Byron had died at Missolonghi in the fight against the Turks. His memory in Greece had lingered on. Athens held the answer to his quest! Would the Greeks support his cause? Now the Greeks were about to meet a man who had another cause to revive: an ancient tradition which was close to their hearts.

***

Architect plans for the re-construction of the
The Acropolis, Athens

CHAPTER 11

GREECE 1895

So great a share of the lovely things of Hellas
Is theirs, let God not envy them
And change their fortune.
Though God alone never tastes woe,
Yet that man is happy and poets sing of him,
Who conquers with hand or swift foot
And wins the greatest of prizes
By steadfastness and strength

PYTHIAN X

Classical painting of The Acropolis

It was a glorious day when they arrived in Piraeus. The white sails of fishing boats moved across the sea like the wings of giant birds. The collection of whitewashed buildings and ancient monuments created an idyllic image.

Vikelas was waiting for Pierre and Marie at the gangplank. His greeting was warm and courteous. The ride by carriage from Piraeus into Athens was delightful. Vikelas had chosen the most scenic route. When the Acropolis came into view, it was like a large white palace illuminated by naked light.

Vikelas told him that they would meet at noon the following day with the Prime Minister. Then he conducted him to the site of the Parthenon. The walk up the hill was long and exhausting. Pierre and Marie felt they were entering into another world. Vikelas explained the fate of the temple and the original scheme of decoration. He pointed out the Panathenic Procession, the sculpted frieze that was one hundred and sixty metres in length. There were the ninety two Metopes representing the battles with centaurs and other mystical scenes. Vikelas told them about the golden and ivory statue of the goddess Athena.

***

It was here that Athena, daughter of Zeus, goddess of Peace and Wisdom, was worshipped. A giant statue had been built in ancient times in her honour and housed in the Acropolis. Athena represented peace, love and knowledge. Her birth was an extraordinary event. Zeus had taken the goddess Meris to his bedroom. Instead of kissing her he swallowed her head, then her body. She was already pregnant and her foetus became detached from her body. It became lodged in Zeus's brain. As the foetus began to grow within his head, the cranium began to swell; when it kicked it caused considerable pain. At the Trito river Zeus appealed to Hephaestos to split his head open with an axe.

This he did; and the Goddess Athena was born.

Athena was born with part of Zeus's wisdom. The golden age of Greek civilisation looked to her benign influence. It was an age in which the foundations of western civilisation were laid. Socrates, Plato and Aristotle were all inspired by this cultural enlightenment.

***

By the end of the day, Pierre and Marie were completely exhausted. In the heat of the night this exhaustion overtook them. Athens was bathed in light, like a jewel encircled by harbour and mountains. Their spirits now were overcome by the beauty of the place.

***

The following morning Vikelas informed Pierre of developments in Greek politics which could affect his plans. There was already an existing Olympic Committee in Greece, named after Zappas. Its chairman was a Mr. Dragounis. Vikelas had friends on this committee. He was aware that these members supported the present Prime Minister, Tricoupis. The Prime Minister, however, was locked in a power struggle with Prince Constantine. For this reason the Olympic Committee was opposed to an Olympics in Athens.

Pierre was introduced to George Melas, son of the mayor of Athens who supported his plan. He also met with Alexander Mercati, son of the director of the Ionian Bank.

They told him of the excellent facilities for the proposed games: the Zappeion rotunda, excellent for fencing and equestrian events; Phaeleros Bay for yachting and rowing; and the bay of

Zeos for swimming and diving.

***

Pierre found the Prime Minister, Mr Tricoupis, warm and friendly. He smiled easily at Pierre and welcomed him. He was introduced to the other dignitaries. The room was on a grandiose scale. It had an enormous number of tapestries and paintings. There was lavish plaster work on the ceiling. The marble floor, with inlays of the colour lavender, gave the room a cool and delicious effect. The Prime Minister spoke. A slight change of tone in his voice indicated that Pierre's proposals were to be discussed.

With the greatest respect, we have read your letter and have spoken to Mr Vikelas. We understand your great desire for the revival of the Games here in Greece, but we consider that the whole scheme is impractical at this point in time. In the light of the present economic climate, it is madness. Greece is bankrupt. We cannot afford to finance such a project. It would cost in the region of a million drachmas. Our political enemies would devour us. Many years ago Zappa tried to revive the Games, but he did not succeed."

Pierre responded." Sir, I do not come alone. I come on behalf of the Olympic Congress. Many nations have joined, expressing their hope for these Games."

The Prime Minister replied. "Yes, we perfectly understand that all of us would dearly love to see the Games here; it would be a revival of part of our ancient culture. But, Monsieur de Coubertin, it is a financial impossibility to stage such an event at this present time."

"But, Sir, we can recover the cost through private subscriptions, and also through the inflow of foreign currency. It will be very worthwhile for Greece staging the Games!"

Tricoupis cut him short. It was as if he was irritated to be told anything on the subject of finances.

"I've studied the costs, it is too expensive. Your ideas are based on respect for our noble past; the Greece of today is different. There have been centuries of oppression. Sometimes those marvellous ancient ideals are a burden on our shoulders. We cannot live in the past. The Games are a splendid idea: personally I give them my warmest support, yet our government can do nothing in this matter."

There was nothing more for Pierre to say; Tricoupis had spoken. The plan of directly financing the project with government assistance was impossible. He thanked the Prime Minister for his courtesy and patience and quietly left.

Pierre left the government buildings, filled with sadness. The city had been brought to a standstill by the heat of the sun. The streets were virtually empty. He remembered how he had listened to the last remarks of Tricoupis in silence. His despondent mood lasted until morning. He recalled the words of his father, "It will be a disaster." Marie consoled him, but she could not lift his depression.

No matter how he went over the matter in his mind, he could see no way forward. The government of Greece had dismissed his idea. They had weighed up the possible political gains or losses and decided to reject his proposal. Tricoupis had just been polite.

***

Pierre received a letter from Tricoupis the following day.

Monsieur le baron... It will be easy for you to understand how strong is our regret at having to decline an honor graciously offered to our country and to lose at the same time an opportunity to associate our efforts with those of elite men who preside over the work of restoring a glorious ancient institution. Aware of the feeble means presently at the disposal of the Greek people and convinced that the task exceeds our resources, we haven't had the liberty to choose.

Pierre was tired, his mind strayed so much that he didn't even know the time of day. He had not opened the shutters of the room since he entered. He was exhausted.

He was asleep when Vikelas came to the door. Dazed, he answered the door. There was a look of intense distress on Vikelas's face.

"Tricoupis will gain no friends from his actions today, Pierre." "It seemed so final. What is there for me to do now except return to Paris?"

"No, you must not return. Wait here for a few days in Athens. I want to work out a new plan."

"But the Greeks have refused. What can I do? Without Greece it would not be the same."

"But you cannot give up now, Pierre. You are exhausted and tired."

"Pierre, I am so sorry, but there are others in Greece who can help. I know from Palace sources that Prince Constantine is very excited at the prospect of holding the Games. The whole Royal family would be pleased to have this great symbol resurrected. Greece needs this ideal again."

"Yes, we met him at the Congress, but I had not thought of requesting him to become directly involved."

"You know, it was King George who sent a cup for the victors to Dr. Brooke at Much Wenlock. He would be most satisfied to think that Greece might stage an international games."

"What can be arranged?" asked Pierre.

"Please leave it to me, Pierre. I will make the necessary arrangements. It is imperative that you speak with Prince Constantine," said Vikelas.

"We must act quickly. There is a danger of bad publicity in the newspapers. In France it would be a personal disaster for me. I can imagine my father's reaction."

"The meeting this morning was private. Tricoupis has reasons not to have his response publicised. I will come tomorrow and tell you what has been arranged. Remember, not a word to anyone," replied Vikelas.

As night descended on Athens, up on the great hill Pierre could see the beautiful illuminated crown of the Acropolis. He could not think of the future without fear. The ancient spell, however, of Athens lifted his spirits. He felt the cool breeze of the evening which spread through the streets and along the distant hills. He would sleep long and hope fervently, for his own future and the future of the Games hung in the balance.

***

Tricoupis the Greek Prime Minister declared Greece bankrupt
in 1893 and refused to support
De Coubertin's revival of the games.

CHAPTER TWELVE

ATHENS 1895

He shall surpass all men
In prophecy to dwellers on earth,
And his race shall never fail.
Now you shall hear a voice that knows not lies,
And when Herakles, the bold deviser, comes,
A holy shoot from Alkaios' sons,
And founds a feast of many men
For his Father and orders the greatest of Games,
You shall set up an oracle
On the topmost altar of Zeus.

OLYMPIAN

The Greek Royal Family in 1890

Pierre arrived with Vikelas and Marie at the palace. It was bathed in the golden evening light. Its classical arches cast strong shadows across the lawn. The palm trees swayed in the cool evening breeze. The architecture belonged to the finest classical traditions. Pierre could observe the coat of arms of the royal family over the doorway. He entered a large vaulted patio covered in mosaic tiles. A young man stood talking to an older woman, who was taking tea on the terrace.

Vikelas informed him that it was Prince Constantine, with his mother Queen Olga. The prince noticed their arrival and hurried along the patio to greet them. Pierre observed the fine features of the Prince. He had a shock of blond hair and an athletic figure. He was well tanned and by all accounts seemed to lead a sporting life.

The Prince greeted them warmly. His royal lineage had withstood all the trials of Greek history. Now Greece was basking in the glory of independence, which it had so dearly won from the Turks. The Prince sat with them both all afternoon in his drawing room. He was sharp and quick-witted. He was intrigued by Pierre's idealism. He had not heard of his meeting with Tricoupis, but was not surprised by the result. If his government was not interested in culture it was up to people in exalted positions to support worthy causes. The Prince would help him weave his way through the complexities of Greek political life. He was beginning to understand that reviving the Olympics was not just about the revival of ancient culture, but was about re-establishing the noble qualities of the human spirit.

The Prince spoke energetically. He rejected Tricoupis's opinion. He felt that the whole problem of costs could be resolved by a single financier. In the meantime a national collection could begin.

The Prince stood silently, looking out across the lawns of the Palace. His face seemed sculpted in the golden evening light. He mused for a moment, then turned gracefully.

"There is only one man that can save this operation. Georgias - yes, Georgias Averoff! We must meet him as soon as possible."

Georgias Averoff! Pierre had not heard of him before. He learnt that he was a philanthropist and a man of enormous wealth who lived mostly in Alexandria in Egypt. He was a man reputed to be as wealthy as any American railroad magnate.

The Prince appointed a committee of twelve men. The date of the opening of the Games was set for the following year, on the National Day of Independence. The deep significance of this day within the national life of Greece could not be overlooked. The Prince made the suggestion to change the names of the streets from Turkish and Venetian back to Greek. It was clear now to Pierre that the royal family saw it as their duty to promote the Games in the life of all the Greek people.

***

With a tremendous sense of mystery Pierre and Marie travelled to the villa, along the coast, where a meeting had been arranged with Averoff. The villa overlooked the pale blue Aegean. Across the waters lay the island of Hydra. Out there had sailed the Greek ships from Troy, home to their beloved country. The villa was not unlike a Greek temple, with statues of ancient goddesses. They stood serene and beautiful in a surreal kind of way, as if paying homage to the past. Some peacocks strutted across the courtyard and drank at the fountain. It was an idyllic scene, illuminated by the golden light of the early evening sun. Pierre observed a large rock sitting across the mouth of the harbour below, barren and brown against the perfect blue. Beyond was a long cliff face of orange with brown flecks. The surrounding green-blue water was as smooth as a highly bronzed mirror.

When they came closer he could see an imposing mansion. A small stone wall surrounded the house. The entire front faced the sea. The arches were of marble. Rows of fir trees and cypresses penetrated the clear sky. The image was not unlike Bocklin's painting of the 'Isle of the Dead'.

Pierre was received at the gate with bows and handshakes by one of the servants and led up the winding pathway. Under one of the colonnades stood Averoff wearing a white silk suit. He had the colour of one used to bathing in the sun. He was large in build, a man in his seventies with greying hair. He sported a beautifully shaped moustache.

"Welcome! I am delighted to meet you, Monsieur de Coubertin," said Averoff, nodding his approval. "I have heard from Constantine about your grand project."

Pierre introduced Marie. Averoff bowed to Constantine. Then they entered the house. They sat in large armchairs by the window overlooking the sea.

The interior of the house was neo-classical in style with French decorative motifs. The Sevres porcelain plates on the dining room table had pictures of the Sphinx. On the wall hung a vast tapestry. It depicted a hippopotamus on the river Nile, with reeds, and a large standing stork.

"Tell me, what do you think it will cost?" said Averoff, puffing his cigar.

"So far, through the national collection and the money raised on the stamp issue we have raised sixty thousand drachmas. The entire cost is estimated at close to a million drachmas," said Pierre.

"Ah yes, you need to build a stadium."

"Yes, we can reconstruct the old stadium in Athens. Without that there can be no games."

"I have learnt that the Prime Minister does not approve.""Yes," said Pierre nervously.

"He has always been the same. He doesn't understand! A country without its past is nothing. In Egypt the past is preserved. Look at the Pyramids. Much of the origin of Greek culture lies there. Now, to business, what can I do for you'? asked Averoff.

"Well, to be extremely blunt, we have reached a crisis point with regard to this project," said Pierre.

"Nonsense, my boy, one is never in a crisis - one should always anticipate disaster."

"Monsieur Averoff, a date has already been set for the Games. Yet we have only collected ten per cent of the finance at this stage. We should ask you for help. You are held in very high esteem by the Greeks," said Constantine quite formally.

"You flatter me, Constantine, it is just that at various times I have dabbled in Greek affairs. I would rather like to think I can be of assistance in these difficult times."

"Yes, the cost is estimated at one million drachmas. I thought perhaps ... you might be prepared to help us," said Pierre.

Averoff got up and walked up and down the long room. He

stood and gazed at the patterned ceiling, deep in thought. He then turned and addressed them.

"You are surrounded by a civilisation that was built by men of vision. Out there lie great temples - a vast civilisation, more complex than we can imagine. Your idea, Pierre, is fixed in your mind. Millions of ideas have been conceived over the centuries like drops in the ocean. But each idea must be nurtured like a flower. You have proposed the most wonderful idea. You are reviving something which has been dead for a long time. Your plan, Pierre, is to recreate something of great value and relight the flame of peace. History will be rewritten and generations hereafter will be thankful."

As he finished speaking, a beautiful young girl with blonde hair and blue eyes entered the room. It was Averoff's daughter Helena.

"Helena, my dear," said her father, welcoming her.

"Oh, I'm sorry, father. I didn't know you had visitors."

"Helena, I want you to meet some friends of mine, Baron Pierre de Coubertin, his wife Marie and Prince Constantine."

"My pleasure," said Helena.

"Come and join us, my dear."

Then Averoff turned to Pierre.

"If it presents no difficulties for you, I would like to pay for the cost of the stadium. Whatever other money you raise over and above can be used to extend hospitality to the guests who will arrive. Greece needs the games, she needs the inspiration of

Olympia. You want to create something of great value in the world. If money is the only obstacle, it will be removed."

Averoff rose and tugged at a tasseled rope. A moment later one of the servants entered, carrying a silver tray which was placed in front of him. On it lay a draft, drawn on the bank in Athens. Averoff filled in the details and signed it. It sat there, a green and white piece of paper with the figure written out in full.

"Let me propose a toast: To Pierre de Coubertin and the dream that is soon to come to life."

Pierre silently remembered the music of the Hymn to Apollo and thought of the words 'God loves what is best in human nature.'

Pierre was elated. This time the pendulum had swung in the opposite direction. A great and wonderful breakthrough had been made. It was as if he had visited Zeus and made a request at Mount Olympus, and the Gods had granted him his wish. Averoff had extraordinary resources, that was certain.

"It has long been a cherished idea of mine to revive Greek culture, but the plan for the Games, embracing as it does all nations, is really a superb one. It should, however, be carried out with as little delay as possible," said Averoff, drawing on his cigar.

"Pierre, you are the one that has believed faithfully. You have sincerely tried to establish this great and noble project and now you will succeed."

They all stood and raised their glasses.

"To a dream that is about to come to life."

Helena threw her arms around her father and kissed him.

"I knew you would help, Georgias, you have never let me down. You are a fine man. Now, we must return to work, I look forward to seeing you in Athens before too long," said the Prince.

"Here it is! It's like a miracle... one million drachmas. Send it to the treasury at once and announce it to the committee. Announce it to the nation and the world... The Games are on" said Pierre with great excitement, jumping to his feet.

***

In Paris at the de Coubertin house Pierre's father was having breakfast. The Baroness rushed in with a newspaper.

"0h, Charles, have you seen the paper this morning?" said the Baroness excitedly.

"The Games are going to take place next Easter in Athens. Pierre has raised one million drachmas."

"Well, that's the best game of poker I've seen in a long time..." replied the Baron, glancing up from his newspaper in a state of astonishment.

***

Pierre wrote to Dr. Brooke that evening. The doctor's dream had come true. Pierre however realised, sadly, that the good doctor would never he able to come to Greece.

Dr. Brooke was elated at the news that Pierre had won through. As he sat in his garden that very afternoon he reflected on the triumphs and struggles of his own life, and the days he had spent with Pierre. Now his life-long dream was about to become a reality.

Throughout the world newspapers carried the message, 'The Olympic Games revived'.

***

Georgios Averoff, the greek Billionaire who paid for the rebuilding of the Olympic stadium. Prince Constantine along with Philemon (Secretary General of the Olympic Games) and De Coubertin, persuaded him to financethe whole project

CHAPTER THIRTEEN

OLYMPIA 1895

We shall set golden pillars
Under the chamber's well-made porch
And build, as it were, a marvellous hall;
When work is begun,
The front must be made to shine afar.
If there were an Olympian victor,
Steward at Pisa of God's oracular altar
And founder's kin to glorious Syracuse,
What hymn would that man not have
If he found his townsmen
Unstinting in songs that he loves?

PYTHIAN X

Olympia, the ancient stadium where the original games were located

Pierre and Marie left Athens for a number of days. Pierre was anxious to see for the first time the place of his dreams, Olympia. Olympia was not just a physical location. It was the loveliest ancient site in all Hellas. It had green wooded hills which were surrounded on all sides by smiling plains. The sky seemed to cast its light into the river which flowed through it. Across from the deep valley was the low hill of Kroniom. To the south the great river of Alphaes descended from the mountains. Its winding, gurgling waters broke against white pebble-covered inlets.

Since ancient times men had searched among the ruins of this neglected site. The first excavations were at the Temple of Zeus in 1829 by a French expedition. The ground plans of the temple was revealed. Some of the sculptured panels that were excavated were placed in the Louvre.

It was the Morea expedition, carried out by the Frenchman Albert Blouet in 1828, that made the first significant discovery of the Temple of Zeus.

In 1874 the German Curtius explored it systematically with the backing of Kaiser Wilhelm. This archaeologist had helped excavate the site of the original stadium.

Here at the temple of Zeus Pierre made a discovery which would come to symbolise the Olympics. He found five interlocking rings covered in sand. Pierre wiped the sand away and knelt thinking for a moment, perhaps these rings could one day signify the unity of all the continents and became the Olympic symbol.

The temple stood at the south-west corner of Alpheus. Phidias the sculptor had designed the statue of Zeus, which was regarded as one of the seven wonders of the world. Made of gold and ivory, Zeus sat on his throne and held a figure of Nike, Goddess

of Victory, in his right hand, and a sceptre in his left. The altar of Zeus, built by Libon of Elis in 460 B.C., was sited near the Temple of Hera which was built in 600 B.C., the oldest temple in Olympia. Nearby was the sacred grove of wild olives. Branches had been cut from it to weave the Olympic victor's crown.

Every Greek considered it a great misfortune to die without having seen the statue of Zeus. Phidias had depicted Zeus as a mighty sovereign and loving father, calm and serene, mild and benevolent. In the little group was a handsome youth full of vitality. His image was one of young manhood, supple with strength, the ideal youth which the Greeks adored.

The Actis was the sacred grove of Zeus, an irregular quadrangle more than 200 yards long. To the north was the Hill of Kronos. Within encased walls were the Temples of Zeus and Hera where votive offerings were made. Outside were administration buildings, hostels, visitors' accommodation and baths.

In the ancient Olympics there were four running events: the stade, a sprint of about 200 meters; the diaulos, which was two stades or about 400 meters; the dolichos, 20 to 24 stades in length, or approximately 4000 to 5000 meters long; and the hoplite race, which was a diaulos in distance.

The games were organised into a series of events, most notably (lie contest for trumpeters, heralds, boys, horse races, the pentathlon then the rites for Pelops, the sacred procession and the great sacrifice to Zeus. Afterwards came the crowning of the victors. There was also a banquet of the participants and the sacrifice in the prytaneion.

The Games were carried out under the guidance of the Olympic laws known as leges sacrae. These concerned the sanctuary, sacrifice and worship of Zeus. The rules of the Games were governed by the judges, known as the Hellenodikai. Their word was final and absolute.

Olympia was more than anything Pierre's imagination had ever conjured up. It was a place where the truce had been observed. Once every five years the heralds went out and announced the beginning of the Games. When contestants travelled from all over Greece the truce ensured their safe passage.

All of Greece gathered in this valley. An event was celebrated in supreme acts of human endeavour. Olympia was the valley of peace. Athletes and pilgrims convened at the sacred site. It was a demonstration of that aspiration which transcended all conflicts; men came together, united by the will of the Gods.

To break the truce destroyed one's participation in the Games: the Olympics without it was a betrayal. Imposing the sacred truce ensured that only men of peace would come to the altar of Zeus. This was the ideal behind the Games.

The poet Pindar wrote his odes there. For Pindar victory in the Games raised questions of mystical and metaphysical importance. Glory was something which came from the Gods, and athletes became immortal in the moment of triumph.

For much of their time men led a shadowy existence, but when the gods sent a divine brightness everything changed. Pindar evoked the triumph beyond ordinary emotions that transformed men's lives. The Greeks believed that winning came from the Gods. The Gods were everywhere. Men were nothing compared with them, for this reason the poet's task was to catch and keep the fleeting divine moment: to reveal to men what really was important in their lives. Pindar believed that men became immortal when they won at the Olympian games. Pierre for the first time was beginning to understand Olympism. As he looked across the plains of Olympia with Marie and observed the setting .sun, he knew now that his quest was nearly over.

***

There were vivid entries in Pierre's diary of this visit.

"I remember the footpath that climbed snakelike up the little hill where the museum and hotel were located. A pure air, perfumed with scents, blew up from the banks of the Alpheus. For a moment the moonlight animated a vaporous landscape, then a starry night fell over the two thousand years with which I had come to seek stirring contact." Because of the hour, "I was forced to wait until dawn to discern the outlines of the sacred landscape of which I had so often dreamed."

The next day from my window, I kept watch for the sunrise, and as soon as its first rays had crossed the valley, I rushed toward rite ruins. Their smallness - owing on the one hand to the restrained proportion of the buildings and, on the other, to their crowdedness (this absence of open spaces so characteristic of Greek and Roman civilisation, which is in striking contrast to Persian conceptions) - neither surprised nor deceived me. It was a moral architecture I was going to gather lessons from, and it magnified every dimension. My meditation lasted all morning while only the noise of the bells of the flocks on the way to Arcadia disturbed the silence. All morning long I wandered in the ruins."

***

Pierre approached the entrance of the Prytaneion. This was

where the "Prytaneis" the sacred officials of the sanctuary were located. He walked slowly towards the special room where the eternal flame once burned. There, he silently vowed that it would be lit again.

***

NIKE, GODDESS OF VICTORY.

Nike, Goddess of Victory, the greeks believed that Nike joined their athletes in their strugge for Victory

CHAPTER FOURTEEN

AMERICA 1895

Many were the leaves and the garlands
They threw on him,
And many the wings of victory
He had won before.

PYTHIAN IX

James Connolly, son of Irish Famine immigrents from the Arran islands of the west coast of Ireland, the first Olympic gold medal winner.

As Pierre walked through the wooded hills of Olympia, many thousands of miles away a young American was about to become involved in an adventure that would change his life. James Connolly was of Irish descent. He lived near Harvard University, but in one of the district's poorer quarters. His parents were proud of their son. They had sacrificed much to send him to university, a fact Connolly was made painfully aware of. Sometimes he wished that he could leave the university and take up some paying job. He seemed to take more of an interest in sport than in his studies. The Dean's reports demonstrated that if he did not work harder he would fail his degree. Connolly realised that he was no academic. He liked being out in the open air, cutting wood or bricklaying. His father had been a labourer too. He had come over on the great exodus from Ireland. He often spoke of the Island of Dreams, Ellis Island, where millions of Irish immigrants had passed through. He was one of the two million Irish who had crossed the Atlantic, in search of a better future.

This great exodus had begun after the 1847 famine when the potato crop failed. Millions died and the population was reduced from eight million to three. Connolly's father was nostalgic about Ireland, like many of the Irish that had come to America: nostalgic for the beautiful green land where life was simple and people warm and friendly. He would speak to James late into the night about his country, a country that James had never seen.

James felt American, but at times he sympathised with his father who felt the pain of the emigrant, forever in exile. Some had chosen this exile but others had had it forced upon them. It was his ambition to return to his beloved land one day.

He had come over with the Costelloes and the Kellys from Philadelphia. They had come from Westport in Mayo. Not far from there was Knock, where the Virgin Mary had appeared. His father often spoke of his religious convictions and the necessity for prayer. He never failed to attend Sunday Mass, and James was obliged to visit his local church to attend whenever he was home from college.

His mother was more light-hearted than his father. She laughed a lot and often made fun of her husband's nostalgia, even though she was of Irish descent too. She felt that all the Irish talked about was of returning to Ireland. But they never did.

James often lay in the hammock on his terrace and dreamed. Sometimes the wind swept through the timber-framed house and he could hear it creaking as if it was speaking to him.

James rarely received letters at home. When his mother arrived with a letter he opened it quickly.

"It's from Robert Garrett, some fat cat up at Princeton ... He wants me to go to Athens, to run in the Olympics," James informed his mother.

"Athens is a long way off ... Who's going to pay for it? Harvard costs us enough already," replied his mother, bitterly.

"Yes, mam ... but it would be great to run for America!"

"Now, Jamie ... don't start getting ideas into your head. We sacrificed everything to get you into Harvard ... Do you know how difficult it was for your father when he came over from Ireland, after that dreadful famine?"

"I agree ... but an Olympic run for America could do a lot for my career."

James did not discuss the matter further with his mother. He needed time to think. He had never heard of Robert Garrett before, but he had met some of the boys from Princeton. Most of them were rich kids and quite arrogant. He felt that they had little backbone on the sports track. He usually ran them into the ground. They had no nerve for competition, they were born with a silver spoon in their mouth. At least, it seemed that way when they hit the track and Connolly sped ahead. Connolly felt that he had to prove a point. These Princeton boys might be richer and more privileged, but he was still faster than them.

His father's ambitions for his son had influenced him. If he could not become a great academic, he could certainly be a great athlete. Connolly fell asleep in the hammock that afternoon as the sun set. He could not have known that in Boston Sloane was already making moves to raise money for the first American Olympic team.

***

Sloane could be found at one of Boston's gentlemen's clubs. He sat on a leather chair, smoking cigars and talking with Arthur Burnham and Oliver Ames, governor of Massachusetts, two of Boston's notable financiers. The two men were sceptical at first. Sloane continued to talk to them in a persuasive manner.

"I've brought you chaps together because I want you to finance the American team," quipped Sloane, pulling on his cigar.

"Yes, but is it going to happen?... I read the other day that de Coubertin is still looking for Greek support," interrupted Ames.

"Of course it's going to happen"? said Sloane.

"How much do you need ?" asked Burns.

"Well, I'm planning on an eight man team. I need money to cover training, runners, tracksuits ... the ship tickets, accommodation ... let's say $140,000."

"Can we both come?" Ames asked, looking at Burnham.

"Why, of course ! If we win some golds for America, it will be worth it. You will have a reputation ... Think of the publicity!"

"I'm not so sure if it's a wise investment," said Burns, warily.

"Look, every day we invest in the stockmarket, on futures and options; that's what I call a poker game. Let's just go for it?" said Ames, pausing for a moment, looking intently at Burns.

"OK, Sloane, you're a very persuasive man."

Sloane sprang from his chair, extending his hand to both men.

"I won't forget you for this, boys. America will be proud of you.

"By the way, I know a good cross country runner in Boston ... his name is Arthur Blake, one of the fastest men in America," Ames informed him.

"Where can I find him?"

"At the Boston Athletics Association, but you'll find him bricklaying with some Irish company called Kellys."

"Well, I must get up there as soon as possible."

Sloane was pleased to have secured the two bankers' approval so quickly. He sent a letter to Garrett, who was beginning to put a team together. Garrett had already received confirmation from

Arthur Blake of the Boston Athletics Association, who agreed to attend a track meeting at Princeton.

He had not received a reply from Connolly; by now he was becoming impatient. Sloane would be back in a few days and he wanted a team up and ready to train. Bert Tyler, his best friend, agreed also to take part in the training. He told Garrett that he would try and talk Jameson, one of the best sprinters, into the idea. Garrett was pleased to learn that his father had agreed to foot the bill for the entire Princeton team.

***

Early one morning Robert and Bert made their way to the train station. They took a trip down to Harvard to try and locate Connolly. Bert assured him that it was worth getting this Irishman involved. At the porter's office they were informed that Connolly could normally be found at the gym.

***

Garrett found Connolly there, lifting weights. It seemed at any moment his heart would burst from his chest. Connolly gritted his teeth and struggled with the great weights. After a further series of presses, he put the barbell to rest on his bench. It was only when he sat up that he discovered that Garrett and Tyler were there.

"My name is Garrett. Did you get my letter?"

"Yeah, sure," said Connolly.

"Well, what do you say?"

"No deal ... I can't go to Athens," replied Connolly, covered in sweat.

"Why not?"

"Because I ain't got the money. I don't come from a rich family like you boys. My parents are poor Irish emigrants."

"Money is no problem. Professor Sloane from Princeton has raised the capital. My father is pitching in too".

"Well, that's a different story!"

"What do you reckon?"

"Well, it's not just the money. I'll have to talk some people into the idea. My mother and father, and there's the dean of Harvard ... that boring old idiot. He's always giving me a hard time," said Conolly.

"That should not be a problem ... I'm sure he'll agree ... I've got to get permission, too. Let me talk to him ... I'll get Sloane's support," said Garrett, laughing.

"... and then there's this Irish girl I'm seeing. She will not be too pleased when she hears I'm disappearing for several months."

"Don't worry about the girls. They will be waiting for you when you get back. Right, let's get training ... I've got to meet up with three other fellows from Princeton. I've invited them for a meeting next week."

"But your boys from Princeton couldn't walk a mile, let alone run a race!"

"Look, Connolly, I know that you are a brilliant athlete, but

Princeton's got some fine men too. We need a strong team. We don't want to get run over by the French or the Greeks. We've Sol some of the best trainers and athletes here in America."

"That's me," said Connolly, laughing,"OK, you've got yourself a deal. If I run into any problems with my parents or the dean, I'm dropping out."

"Don't worry, let me handle the problem. You just start training. Now, let's meet up next Sunday, in the pavilion, beside the track," said Garrett enthusiastically.

***

Later that day Connolly strolled down by the lake. He loved the light at that time of the evening, the cool blue light that reflected in the lake. He could see some swimmers making their way across the water. They created slow ripples as they moved gracefully along. He was worried about his new commitment to Garrett. Confronting his parents and the Dean would not be easy. He knew that there was going to be a problem.

He had arranged to meet his girlfriend Elizabeth. She worked nearby in a cafe in the university grounds. He observed Elizabeth with her thin frame and blond curls bobbing across the lawn. Her blue dress shimmered in the sunlight. She beamed a smile at him. Elizabeth was also of Irish extraction. Both families knew each other well. She had the easy going nature of the Irish, in contrast to the snobbish attitudes of her fellow campus girls, who daily checked who could become a member of their private fraternity. Elizabeth was confronted with many questions. What pedigree had their family? What position did they hold in society, and what property did they own? Friendships were like card games to them. Connolly rejected the bourgeois prejudices of the college. Elizabeth did not care for the boys either and she hated their arrogance.

"Look, Elizabeth, it will only be for a couple of months," was Connolly's reply to Elizabeth's reservations about Athens.

"That's what my last boyfriend said ... He went to California, met some girl and never came back ... Oh, James, why do you have to go?"

"Look, don't worry, I'll come back to you, Lizzy. I've not told my parents ... My father will hit the roof."

"You bet ... He's won't spend his money for you to run off to Athens. What's so important about these bloody Games anyway?"

"You would not understand."

"It's pride."

"Yes, it's pride, American pride," said Connolly rather defensively.

"No, it's that stubborn Irish pride you have, you want to prove that you are better than everyone else."

"It will be the finest contest of international sport ever staged. The prize will be an Olympic gold medal."

"What does it matter if you win or lose?"

"If we do, we will have achieved something for ourselves and for America."

Who cares about America? What about us? You're going to

throw everything away, just to become a hero.""Look Elizabeth, this is a difficult decision for me. Please try to understand," said Connolly as he got ready to leave. I He felt a little hurt by her indifference to his plans. He had to admit that he was bitten by the Olympic bug.

***

Connolly had not seen the Dean for some time and it was generally accepted around the campus that he was a difficult man to deal with. He had never received any acclaim for his obscure research on Latin hymns. His position as Dean gave him a certain importance, even though he was looked down upon by the other professors. He felt that he had the last say in any intellectual argument or matters pertaining to the college.

Connolly sat in the Dean's office and waited. He looked around the walls stacked with books of philosophy and literature. There were photographs of all the great men that had passed through these illustrious rooms. The Dean entered swiftly in a frock coat. He had a large handlebar moustache, and his bald domed forehead signified a man of mature years.

He observed the Dean's expression, the wisps of hair, the cold empty stare and the swift movement of his lips. Only the curved lines of his moustache softened his face. His expression gave nothing away of his emotions. The Dean flicked through Conolly's letter.

" I have read your letter, and have considered your request," said the Dean leaning back in his chair.

"I'm sorry, but I can not allow you to go to Athens," he continued sternly, wiping his whiskers.

"Why not?" said Connolly, quite disturbed by his reply.

"Look at it this way, young man. If I gave everyone permission to go on these overseas trips, I would have hundreds of students taking holidays. Connolly, you know that your grades have not exactly been exemplary."

"Surely you can compromise this time. After all, it is the revival of the Olympics."

"Compromise, my boy! I set the policies in this university. If you go to Athens I'm afraid I will have to ask you to leave Harvard. Discipline in one's studies is a priority in this college."

***

Sloane and Garrett received the news with a sense of despair. Connolly would have to make a decision about his future academic career. Sloane approached the Dean the following day, but received the same reply. Connolly sat beside the lake all afternoon trying to decide what to do. If he went to Athens he would lose his girlfriend and his career. He felt that Elizabeth should stand by him, whatever his decision was. The one great obstacle to his plans was his father. When he spoke to him that evening, he received a similar reaction.

***

Connolly travelled up to Princeton to meet Garrett and Sloane. He met with them at the athletics pavilion.

"He's a cantankerous old bugger," said Sloane, leaning back in his chair.

"It's the devil's alternative," replied Garrett.

"That old fool means business."

"Look, James, we can't force you to go to Athens, you know, there's too much at stake. Ultimately it's your decision," said Sloane.

Yes, I know, Professor. It's going to be the most difficult decision of my life."

***

Garrett started practising his discus on the front lawn of his house. Sloane came by to study the emergence of this new Greek hero. Garrett's girlfriend Katherine was enthusiastic about his new ambition. She daily encouraged him to throw the discus further. Katherine was athletic by nature. She would run down the well cut lawn and mark the spot. Sloane would hurry across the grass with his tape and record the distance. Very soon Garrett had thrown the discus beyond all recorded distances. The only worry now was whether they could beat the Greeks at their own game. After all, it was an art that was still practised by some of Greece's finest athletes.

Sloane received confirmation from Pierre that the games were on. There was much elation when he announced this to the newly formed team. Their embarkation from Boston was only a few weeks away and they would have to train hard.

The final line up from Princeton was Robert Garrett Jr. Francis A Lane, Albert Tyler and Herbert Jameson. From the Boston Athletics Association came Blake, Ellery Clark and James Connolly from Harvard, Thomas Burke and Thomas Curtis from Boston University. The rest of the contingent were the marksmen, Summer and John Paine, the swimmer, Gardiner Williams, Princeton trainer Scotty Mc Master, and John Graham, a manager from the Boston Athletics Association.

***

Boston 1896, the great day of departure arrived. The American team were fit and ready. Sloane had negotiated with the ship's captain so they could train on deck. However, the fate of Connolly was on everyone's mind. They had not heard from him for weeks. It was generally accepted that he had dropped out.

The great ocean liner was moored at the Boston docks, hundreds of people had gathered there. A brass band boomed across the harbour. Banners with the American flag flew in the sea breeze. Sloane stepped out of a gleaming carriage with the American ambassador. A line of marines wearing white suits greeted them, bayonets pointing in the air. The ambassador was introduced to Garrett, Tyler, Lane, Jameson and Bourke. Katherine hurried towards the crowds to Robert, kissing him.

"I shall miss you," she said.

"And I will miss you too," said Robert, holding her in his arms and giving her a passionate kiss.

"I'll bring a gold medal back especially for you," he continued."And what has happened to Connolly?" asked the ambassador, turning to Sloane.

"I think we've lost him," replied Sloane.

***

At that moment Connolly's train from Harvard was speeding towards the station in Boston. During the night, on impulse Connolly had dressed quickly, packed his things and taken the early morning train. He had not informed Elizabeth of his departure, but he left a note for his parents. He knew it would be a long time before they would forgive him. He reminded them that they had once taken a ship from Ireland to America, and what a risk and a great adventure it was. He, too, would make such a great leap into the unknown.

***

The America national anthem boomed across the crowd. President Cleveland stepped forward and greeted the American team.

"It is. a proud day for America. Do your best and come back with some golds," said the President, firmly shaking Sloane's hand.

Sloane assured him that he had put together America's finest. The ship's steward came down the gang plank and announced that they were casting off and should soon board ship. Hundreds of people waved their parasols and handkerchiefs to their loved ones. Garrett said good-bye for the last time to Katherine who broke into tears. The sound of the ship's foghorn was heard across the harbour, and they knew that they had to hurry.

Connolly had arrived at the harbour front too. He was now struggling through the crowds milling around the President and t he gangplank. He spotted a tall negro who resembled a Masai warrior, hovering above the crowd.

"Stop the ship! I'm one of the American team!" shouted Connolly.

The negro turned towards one of the sailors and shouted as loud as he could.

"He's one of the team! Let him through!"

Without further ceremony, the enormous negro lifted him onto his shoulders and carried him through the crowds. Sloane and Garrett were standing on deck surprised to see Connolly.

"It's Connolly! He made it!" said Garrett, excitedly.

"Well, I'll be damned!" said Sloane, pulling on his cigar.

"God save America!" replied Garrett, hurrying down the gangplank.

Connolly threw his arms around Garrett.

"I'm proud of you, Connolly. You won't regret your decision," said Garrett, helping him onto the deck. Later curiosity raged above deck. Sloane wanted to know how Connolly had managed it.

"When I told my Dean at Harvard that I was coming to the Games he said he wouldn't let me go, because my grades weren't good enough," Connolly said.

"So, how the hell did you get here?"

"Well, I just told him: 'I'm going to Athens, I'm through with Harvard.' I marched out of college and here I am."

The group roared with laughter. Sloane commented,

"You must have Olympic fever, my boy."

"It's catching like wild fire."

Connolly and the team greeted each other warmly. They knew only too well the sacrifices he had made.

***

In the ship's banqueting room Sloane held court. The ship's captain had ordered champagne for everyone. Someone played ragtime on the piano. Then Sloane got up and proposed a toast."Ladies and gentlemen, I am proud to be here today to see all you fine young men take part in this great adventure. Athens is a long way off. You boys have the possibility to be America's first Olympic heroes. You have all made a sacrifice in one way or another, in taking part in this revival of the Olympic Games. It will create a symbol amongst millions of people and contribute to new and peaceful relations between many countries. It is the world's first true international event. My thoughts and feelings are with you all. I propose a toast now to the Olympic ideal and the American team."

Then the celebrations began. The ladies in their finery took to the floor with their partners. Garrett and the rest of the team soon discovered their new popularity.

The sunlight soon began to fade across the horizon and the ship's lights glowed in the great sea swell. Connolly leaned over the ship's rails and watched Boston fade into the distance. How many millions of people, he thought, had watched this horizon. Now he was returning back across the Atlantic in the path his father had once taken forty years before. Whatever happened in Athens, he would make his father proud and bring back pride to the Irish, a race that had suffered much in the wake of the largest famine of that century.

***

That evening sun began to set as Sloane spotted Connolly on deck and joined him.

"I'm very pleased to see you, James. I did not think that you would make it."

"It was a difficult decision," replied Connolly, continuing to look across the waves.

"What made up your mind?" questioned Sloane.

"There are some things in life that one cannot explain, I suppose. We all want to achieve something great in our lives, ... we all strive for a greater ambition."

"Don't worry, James. You will make America proud and, I'm sure, your parents too."

They spoke no more that evening. The two men leaned on the balcony rails and looked out across the great waters of the Atlantic, which was beginning to swell before them. The ocean was turning from light blue to dark green. Soon the mainland of America would disappear from view, and in time there would appear the beautiful vistas of the old world.

***

Robert Garrett
Captain of the American Team.

CHAPTER FIFTEEN

MISSOLONGHI

Just as the sons of Homer,
Singers of interwoven lines,
Often begin with a prelude to Zeus,
So this man also
Has taken the first installment of victory
In the holy Games
In the far-sung wood of Nemean Zeus.

NEMEAN II

Bishop Yerminos
The man that started the Greek war of Independance.

Painting by Delacroix
Greece amidst the ruins of Missolonghi

In Athens the building of the stadium continued at a rapid pace. Pierre met with Metaxas, the architect, to discuss progress. Giant pieces of marble were hauled into place. Hundreds of workmen toiled late into the evening. Soon the stadium would be ready. Marie persuaded Pierre to take a break. She could see he was exhausted. Tension was increasing: it was just a week away from the opening, but they had no official confirmation of any team's arrivals. They would have to wait.

Pierre and Marie set out to Missolonghi. Pierre had read about .this small coastal town. It was here that Byron, the great English romantic poet, had made his last stand against the Turks, and here he had tragically died.

Pierre could sense that moments in Byron's life echoed his own. The Greeks had seen many men from northern Europe come to these shores in search of their ancient past. From the eighteenth century an ever increasing number of adventurers had arrived. They were willing and eager to delve into Greek history, as if they had had none of their own. Perhaps it was due to rapid industrialisation in their own countries. These men now searched for virgin territories; they yearned for peasant life among the ruins.

Byron surpassed all those who had come in search of Hellenism. On January 5th, 1824, at Missolonghi, he stepped ashore on that very beach where Pierre and Marie now stood. Pierre pictured Byron strutting through the surf, wearing his red uniform and Greek helmet, being greeted by music and singing.

Pierre dug his feet into the sands of Missolonghi beach. He walked along the shore with Marie, holding her hand firmly. She could see that he was lost in thought. The great disc of the sun was descending onto the shimmering sea. He felt the cool water lap around his feet. He stopped in his tracks, turned to Marie and ran his hands through her hair, touched her lips, then kissed her slowly.

"I will always love you, Marie, whatever happens."

"Don't say such things! Everything is going to be allright."

But even the sweet kiss and her kind words did not stop him thinking about his own dilemma. The ever-present worry was whether the Greeks would rise to the occasion. Would all his plans, like Byron's, wither in the sands of time?

Pierre had undeniable parallels with this great poet. Both had engaged in the cause of a Greek revival. However, Byron's heroic career had floundered there. His romantic conception was greater than the possibility of success. Would this be Pierre's fate? Would Greece and this romantic tradition descend like a phoenix into the ashes of disaster?

Pierre and Marie sat now in a small tavern beside the lagoon and drank some local wine. The sun had not quite disappeared and the light flickered across the water's surface, like a sea of gold.

Byron had suffered a similar fate to his friend, the poet Shelley, who had also died tragically two years before. He drowned in the bay at Lerici on the north west coast of Italy. They burned his body in a funeral pyre on the beach.

Byron recorded the event in his diary. 'All of Shelley's body was consumed except his heart, which would not take the flame.' Shelley's heart was preserved in spirits and given to his wife, Mary. Shelley, too, had believed in a Greek revival. He, like Byron, had dreamed of a Golden Age. In the chorus he wrote to Hellas he prophesised,

The World's great age begins anew
The Golden Years return
Heaven smiles, and faith and empires gleam,
Like wrecks of a dissolving dream.
A loftier Argo cleaves the main.

Byron had dreamed of saving Greece from its fate. In dying he would achieve what he had not achieved in his lifetime. Out of this failure rose the immortal spirit of Byron. It was a dream .that echoed in Byron's own words,

Hail generous youth, whom glory's sacred flame Inspires, and animates the deeds of fame.

Byron, too, evoked this image of a sacred flame. These lines echoed in Pierre's thoughts. He looked out over the blue Aegean that evening. He wondered if he would survive all the trials that were ahead of him. Better men had tried and failed. There was no return now, the die was cast.

***

ATHENS

On his return to Athens, it was at Averoff's house that Pierre first heard the news of intrigues against him. Michael Breal had just arrived from Paris, and met him at the Palace and consoled him.

In Athens several members of the Greek government were plotting to remove him from the Games. Nationalism had encroached again upon his ideal. Even though Athens was the most fitting place to revive the Games, Pierre saw them in a wider context. The Games should be brought to the world and beyond Athens. The Greek nationalists were jealous that a Frenchman was now reviving the Games, coupled by the fact that Pierre's vision of the Games was in a wider international context. Athens was just a stepping stone for the Games to be held in another country. But the Greeks believed that if they were to be revived in Greece they should stay in Greece. The plan was to remove Pierre as soon as possible and replace him with the Greek official, Philemon.

The Prince showed concern for Pierre's position. He was surprised to learn of this political opportunism. He had thought that at least the Olympics would be spared all that. Pierre could become another victim of Greek internal politics. Ranks were closing among the nationalists. They would have to move quickly. However, the Prince could not be seen to be involved as he was an impartial member of the royal household. He had developed a fondness for Pierre and he was not going to abandon him now. It had too often been the case that as soon as one had carried out the work on a great idea, someone else had stepped in and claimed the rewards.

Pierre spoke with Constantine at the Palace.

"Tell me, what's the problem?" asked Pierre.

"They're trying to get rid of you, Pierre."

"Why, Your Highness?"

"They're trying to put Philemon in your place. It's nothing to do with you; it's just because you're French."

"But this nationalism is unnecessary. The Games are international," Pierre replied bitterly.

"Hardly. We've got no Germans, no British and although I didn't want to tell you - now - it looks like we've got no Americans either. They haven't turned up," said Michael.

"I don't believe it!" said Pierre. "The Americans left Boston weeks ago."

***

"Look, let's be realistic at this point. If no one comes to the Games it's going to be very embarrassing. There are only a few days left before the opening. We've spent one million drachmas of Averoff's money on rebuilding the stadium. This could be a disaster," said Pierre despondently.

***

Pierre got up and walked out to the terrace. It was only a few days before the opening of the Games. It seemed that he had reached the eleventh hour. A decision had to be made. Marie followed him and tried to console him. The golden sunset hung on the horizon, and the Acropolis stood out in silhouette against the evening sky.

"Marie, I think the time has come to make a decision. Constantine and Averoff are being polite. However if no one's going to come, I may as well call the whole thing off now and save them the embarrassment."

"Please, Pierre, we can sort the situation out, believe me."

"There's nothing left to sort out," said Pierre."All this talk of international co-operation has come to nothing. We've handed the Olympics to them on a plate, but they couldn't even rise to the occasion. It's absolutely unforgivable. I must tell Averoff and Constantine the Games are off."

"Please, darling, don't be depressed. I'm sure we can get things rolling again in a few months from now. It's a setback, not the end of everything," said Marie, looking into Pierre's eyes. His face was so full of sadness.

"I'm not sure, Marie. They all got their invitations; it's taken a lot of work and organisation, how can we build it all up again? And where the hell is that American, Sloane? He seemed so full of enthusiasm".

"Michael and Prince Constantine are checking the situation, they've sent telegrams."

"But Marie, we've only got two days left. It would take a miracle for them all to turn up now. Maybe father was right after all, and I've gambled too much on this. I believed too much in the ideal. I forgot that I was dealing with human weaknesses."

***

The following day Constantine and Michael met in the vaulted room of the palace to discuss the situation."We've got to sort these Games out," said Constantine.

"I know. Pierre is on the verge of a nervous breakdown. We will have to take action."

"I agree, Your Highness. We've got take this issue out of the domain of politics. It looks like we'll have to postpone the Games anyway for six months. Maybe by then we'll have sorted these problems out.'

***

Pierre received a letter from the Comte De Paris in England.

Pierre was having breakfast with Michael Breal when the letter arrived. It brought news that deeply saddened him.

"Dear Pierre,

I'm afraid this letter brings you sad news. Dr. Brooke passed away late last night. He died at about two o'clock. He was saddened that he was not able to come to Athens and see his great dream come to life. He died knowing that you had achieved his ambition. He spoke of the sacred truce, of the sacred cup, of the golden flame; of men laying down arms in the cause of peace. He spoke fondly of you. You were like his son. His life's work was not in vain. The golden flame is to be at last rekindled. I hope this news does not upset you too much, on the eve of such a great event.

My warmest regards,

The Comte."

Pierre was saddened by the news. He sat for a moment and said a prayer for his old friend.

He remembered sitting with Dr. Brooke, and recalled his entire physical presence. One remembers someone's face, a gesture, a way of moving, an introduction, a small eccentricity, a characteristic gaze; but with the good doctor it was the black clothes and the way he sat and smiled to himself. It was five years since he had sat in the home of the doctor in that little village. He remembered the afternoon fondly.

Dr. Brooke had been Pierre's inspiration. He had not lived to see his dream come true, but he had died with the phrase on his lips, 'Long Live Olympia', dying happy and contented, surrounded by villagers whom he had loved. He had attended them from birth to death, and they had loved him for his devotion to them. As for Pierre, he was happy that some weeks before he had been able to announce to Dr. Brooke the news that this great project would go ahead. At Easter 1896, in a stadium reconstructed of Pentelic marble, the Olympic Games would be revived.

***

Up to the last minute, many doubts hung over the Games. In Oxford Robertson, the classicist, had made the decision to come. Yet Oxford were unable to raise a team. It was Lord Ampthill who refused to accept the classless amateur code, because he wanted no workers taking part. He believed that only aristocrats should be allowed to participate in the Games. Robertson did not endorse Ampthill's views; he was going to go, even if England did not want to send an official team.

In Berlin high level meetings, which included the Chancellor, disapproved of German participation. They felt that de Coubertin wanted to insult the Germans who, they claimed, had discovered Olympia and most of what was truly Greek. They, the Germans, and the ancient Greeks, were masters of that great culture. They felt that the French had not forgotten their old hatreds and that they could not compete with them in athletics.

***

At the Palace a page dressed in white entered. The boy announced that the American ambassador had arrived to see the Prince. The doors of the Prince's rooms swung open and the American ambassador appeared.

"The American team are somewhere in Greece," the Ambassador announced.

"I don't believe it! Where the hell can they be?" replied the Prince.

The ambassador was unable to say.

"Still, if your boys can make it by noon tomorrow to the opening ceremony, that changes everything. Put it this way, Ambassador," said the Prince."It's all in the hands of the Gods."

***

On the route from Piraeus to Athens, a steam train sped along the track carrying the American team towards Athens. From the window the American flag flew, with banners reading 'Harvard' and 'Princeton'. Sloane requested a Greek boy serving wine to bring the team to his carriage.

Minutes later, the captain entered with Frank Lane, Bert Tyler, Bert Jameson, Arthur Blake, and James Connolly. Sloane poured champagne and handed it round. They drank to their impending arrival in Athens. Sloane turned to Garrett,

"I'm proud of you, Garrett, you've got the best athletes in all of America. Athens at last!"

As they raised their glasses, a little Greek boy ran in shouting 'Athens! Athens', then he sounded his bugle. Sloane lit his cigar and leant out of the window. He observed Athens coming closer and the Parthenon in the distance. In the fields Greek peasants waved to them. The train sped down the track. It seemed like a mirage in the intense summer heat. Sloane leaned out of the window and looked across the rugged plains of Greece for the first time. It was everything he had dreamed of: a simple peasant life that had not changed for thousands of years. He caught the whiff of wild flowers in the air and the smell of olives. He could see men and women walk along the stony pathways, with baskets on their backs. He could see, too, shepherds herding sheep and from time to time young children watching the great iron horse that belched smoke across the landscape. These people used horses and carts and were unfamiliar with the industrial age that was beginning to change life in Northern Europe. Here was the simple life beneath a crystal blue sky.

Sloane was joined by the team members who leaned out to observe the ancient landscape. He felt a surge of excitement as the train sped its way along the tracks. They had travelled many thousands of miles to take part in this revival. It seemed to him that this train was now journeying back into an ancient past.

It was the telegraph boy near Athens that spotted the American train. Within minutes he had tapped out a message in Morse code to Athens.

***

At the Prince's apartments a telegram was handed to Pierre.

"It's from the American ambassador! The Americans have arrived. They're at the train station."

Pierre was radiant with relief.

"What are we waiting for! Let's go and meet them," said Michael enthusiastically.

The Prince suggested throwing a banquet to welcome them. Pierre threw the telegram in the air and hugged Marie.

"Let's go! The Games are on!"

Everyone climbed into the Prince's carriage and drove off at speed.

***

Outside the train station a brass band played. The American ambassador welcomed his country's team. The Prince with the others rushed up, inviting the team and the ambassador to the welcoming banquet.

"My God, this certainly is a fine welcome, isn't it, Jim?" said Garrett.

The rest of the team disembarked, and James and Robert were greeted by the ambassador.

"Welcome to Athens, boys, we thought you were lost," said the ambassador.

"We are throwing a banquet in your honour tonight. We're inviting all the contestants," said Prince Constantine.

The train station was filled with crowds of people milling around the Americans. The team was surprised to find such a reception. Garrett and Sloane observed the finely- cut bones and tanned skin of the Greeks. They wore broad linen shirts covered in embroidery. The men had large belts around their waists.

"Athens at last," Sloane sighed.
 The American team had arrived safely. They disembarked and made their way through the throng. Some of the older Greeks looked as if they were greeting their long-lost prodigal sons. Connolly and the boys became excited by their simple warmth. They were relieved that their long trip was over.

***

Later on that evening the Royal Palace was filled with tables covered with food, drink and flowers. A group of musicians played Greek music. Prince Constantine spoke.

The banquet at Constantine's palace was quickly organised. It seemed that all the servants and employees of the royal household had suddenly appeared from behind the curtains. On the long white table was laid the finest silver and gold. Everywhere stood vases decorated with Greek statues, holding giant palm leaves, which kissed the ceiling. The evening light danced across the objects on the table. Some of the finest Greek musicians had been summoned to the palace. Homer would have been pleased to sit here and muse on this great event.

The Americans tasted their first Greek wine, and the finest of ouso was brought from the cellar. They silently thanked God for their safe arrival. Pierre was delighted. Here were the fruits of his work, the many months of painstaking organisation was suddenly realised in a flash. The dream was coming to life.

"Congratulations, Pierre, all our troubles are over! Tomorrow is the big day."

"Your Highness, Pierre, may I present Robert Garrett, the captain of the American team," said Sloane.

"I am so pleased to see you, your team has saved the day," replied Pierre.

"Thank you, sir. We're delighted to he here," explained Garrett.

The Prince smiled at Garrett.

"Have you worked out why you were twelve days late?""No" replied Garrett.

"Well, there's a difference of twelve days between the Julian and Gregorian calendars. Did you not know the world has two time zones?"

Everyone laughed with astonishment with this news. Michael came hurrying up to the group.

"Guess what? Two English competitors have turned up after all, the Germans too, some Australians and an Irishman; in fact, news is coming in that competitors from thirteen countries have arrived and are on their way to the palace."

Marie approached Pierre and kissed him on the cheek."The King, he's arrived with Queen Olga," said Marie. All eyes turned to the giant doors of the ballroom. The King entered wearing a formal military uniform, resplendent in medals. Queen Olga wore a dazzling dress of gold and silk with Creek patterns. Everyone bowed and curtsied as the King and Queen entered.

"Father, it was good of you to come," said Constantine.

"I am delighted to be here, this is of great importance for our country," replied the King with a smile.

Prince Constantine then presented Pierre, Marie, Michael, Averoff and Helena to his parents.

"We have Baron de Coubertin to thank for this great revival," said the Prince.

"Indeed, and I would like to add my personal thanks for all you have done for my country," replied the King.

"Thank you, Your Majesty," Pierre responded."You will always be welcome in Greece," the King replied.

Then the orchestra started to play, as everyone took towards the dance floor. The competitors broke open bottles of champagne and proposed many toasts.

The King sat with Pierre and Marie and they talked late into the evening. Pierre informed him about Olympic history and spoke of Dr. Brooke, whom the king had corresponded with. Then Pierre requested one of the servants to bring the sacred cup of Olympia. Moments later he returned and handed the cup to Pierre.

"I would like, if I may, to present you with this .. a prize for the Marathon."

"This is beautiful," said the King.

"Your Majesty, it is the reason why I am here. This was given to me many years ago by Dr. Brooke. He was a great man, a man with a dream of reviving the Olympics. He passed that dream on to me with this cup. I promised him that I would make it my life's work to realise his vision. He died a few weeks ago, and never lived to see it happen. I feel that his spirit is still with us. I promised that if ever I met a man worthy of it, I would pass on this cup. It once held the oil for the torch at Olympia, and tomorrow at dawn oil in this cup will re-lit the sacred flame. I can think of no fate more fitting for this cup than to be awarded to the winner of the Marathon."

The King sat silently for a moment and pondered. Then he turned to Pierre.

"Dr Brooke was an extraordinary man, " replied the King

"Greece is forever in his debt."

***

Later, Pierre and Marie stood together on the balcony.

"I do love you so much, Marie. It's been such a struggle, this dream of mine. I couldn't have done it without you."

"And now your struggle has turned to triumph. Are you sure you re ready for it?"

Pierre turned and kissed her, then looked up to the Acropolis. Beneath him Athens was filled with thousands of candles illuminating the windows.

***

Lord Byron fought in the Greek war of independance.
He died at Missolonghi in 1824

The American team arrive in Athens

THE OLYMPIC GAMES

ATHENS 1896

Come, 0 muse, tread
a measure of the sacred choirs; come
to charm our song;
Come to see the waiting crowds,
assembled here in their thousands.

ARISTOPHANES

The flame is lit at Olympia

The first day of the Athens Games

Acropolis beyond the new Olympic Stadium

The Games Begin
The King and Queen sat in a marble throne.

King George

Olympia

Just before dawn in Olympia three young women stood before a marble altar. As the sun rose, oil was poured from the sacred cup into a bowl. A shaft of light passed through a lens mounted on a staff, then it struck the oil in the bowl, which burst into flames. Then a maiden stepped forward and lit a torch from the flame.

***

Athens

It was 1896, Easter Sunday in Athens, the eve of the Olympic Games. The weather was overcast and rain threatened. The city of Athens was celebrating Easter with the customary solemnity, and preparing for the celebration of National Independence Day, and the opening of the Games.

Despite the weather the Stadium was gleaming, its pentelic marble white and radiant, like that used in the building of the Acropolis. The old stadium, which had lain so long in ruins, was now a new and worthy site for the staging of the Games. Averoff was popularly deemed to be its saviour. He had contributed so much to the city of Athens, like one of those wealthy medieval princes who sought to save their souls by leaving their fortunes to the Church.

The throng of people began to move along the city streets towards the gleaming stadium. The first ritual was to unveil the Statue of Averoff by Voustrous. Like all such rituals it was accompanied by a band and speeches.

Outside the entrance to the stadium, the life size statue with its modest pose was to be unveiled with due pomp and ceremony. The access bridge to the stadium had been widened. Outside, one could see the special guard dressed in tunics of cherry red, black trousers and white helmets. A procession of the guards, bearing their individual standards, passed by. All the trades were

organised in their separate divisions. The everyday world of the city had come to a standstill. The vast crowds came closer to the stadium and pushed forward. Stranger talked to stranger. Coloured handkerchiefs were waved at the passers-by. encouraging them to come and join the throng.

By 11 o'clock the members of the Royal Household arrived, with Princes George and Nicholas and the Secretary General of the Olympic Council, Timleon Philemon. The rain began to fall, at first a trickle but it became more insistent, until it was a spring shower. The speakers' phrases wafted across the strong breeze, and the heavy rain punctuated their words. At times the speaker seemed like a dumb show piece. Even the children made frantic movements of imitation. The crowd applauded.

Then the Crown Prince rose to speak. Thousands of ears were visibly strained. People no longer kept their heads bowed against the elements. Umbrellas slowly rose all around. The Prince spoke. A great silence fell across the stadium.

"It is due to the well known act of generosity of the great patriot, Georgias Averoff, that the renovation of the Panathenian stadium has come about, a work which gives a national character to the revived Olympic Games."

The applause was deafening and perfectly orchestrated, for as soon as the Prince began to form the words of the next sentence the crowd fell silent.

"Georgias Averoff is worthy of national gratitude for all he has done for us. I know that I am complying with the national wish by honouring him. It was decided that this statue should be erected by money collected from all the Greeks. I wish that the great patriot may live long, to the good of his country. I consider it a great honour to unveil this statue."

The silk ribbon, which held up the blue and white flag covering the statue, was pulled. The work, which had been carried out in the greatest secrecy, was now publicly acclaimed.

Then Mr. Kemeny, member of the International Olympic Committee, stepped forward and placed a laurel wreath at the base, a pedestal without decoration which was inscribed with Averoff's name.

Monday March 25th, 1896, Easter Monday and National Independence Day, was the day set for the opening. Pierre had not slept. The city of Athens had never looked more beautiful, with festive arches everywhere covered in flowers. Hermes Street and Constitution Square was hung with bunting of blue and white. Throughout the city the letters OA (Olympic Association) could be found on posters. The rooftops shimmered with flags and wavering banners.

Could the Greek love of living express itself in such a happy combination of events? Sport, religion and patriotism: the unique combination of the original Olympics had been revived.

Pierre would be the spectator at his own life's ambition. Now he had realised his goal. A whole nation had become caught up in the spirit of the Games. The entire population of a city was approaching the stadium, where over a hundred thousand people would gather.

At 3.30pm. Crown Prince Constantine greeted the King and Queen. The King was dressed in a naval uniform with a gold braided hat. The Queen was dressed in yards of white silk from head to foot. They were both seated on marble thrones, covered with porphyry coloured cushions. The Crown Prince approached the twelve members of his committee: as they had become known, the "apostles". He addressed his father the King and the audience.

"0 King ... Today we see the fulfillment of the International Congress's decision that the first Olympic games should be held in Athens. These games had their birth in Greece fifteen hundred years ago. In order to carry out this decision, whatever was possible was done. I am persuaded that the imperfections of the undertaking will be judged with just indulgence. Through noble contests Greece is closer bound, 0 King, with the rest of the civilised world, in this the very place which involves so many memories, the Panathenian Stadium which has been renovated by the generous patriot, Georgias Averoff.

May it be, 0 King, that the revival of the Olympic Games binds closer the links of mutual affection of the Greek and other peoples. We consider ourselves happy to be the hosts of the Olympic Games. May they bring new life into physical exercise and give us a new moral outlook. I also hope that they contribute to the formation of a new Greek generation, worthy of its ancestors. With these hopes I pray, 0 King, that you graciously agree to declare the opening of the first International Olympic Games."

The King rose and bowed to his son. It was obvious to the stadium, although his voice did not carry beyond a few rows, that the words of the opening were now to be spoken. The great figure of the king, dressed in military uniform, addressed the crowds.

'I declare the opening of the first International Olympic Games in Athens. Long live the nation! Long live the Greek people!"

Within seconds, by an extraordinary acoustic miracle, the entire stadium repeated the last two phrases just uttered by the King,

"Long live the nation! Long live the Greek people!"

The bands had formed in the centre of the stadium and began playing and a choir began to sing the hymn to the Games, composed by Samaras and Palamas.

'Ancient, immortal spirit, unsullied father of that which is beautiful, great and true.'

At first the crowd was slightly out of tune, like a vast congregation. As the song continued the singers became more confident. They readied themselves for the swell and crescendo of the music. The whole stadium exploded with the sound of the hymn of Samaras.

"Descend, make thyself known and shine, hero! On this earth and below these skies, witness of thy Glory, illuminate the endeavour of the noble contests, in the running race, the wrestling and throwing. Place a wreath of evergreen branches. Vales, mountains and oceans shine with thee, like unto a great temple of white and porphyry. All peoples hasten to this temple to worship thee, 0 ancient immortal spirit."

Then everyone looked towards a single maiden dressed in Greek costume holding a torch. She approached a great bowl made of marble. The flames rose towards the sky, as she placed the torch to the bowl. Pierre and Marie stood proudly in the audience. The ancient Olympic flame had been ignited again after fifteen hundred years.

***

The sacred moment had come: the Games were about to begin. Everyone's eyes were focused on the entrance. The contestants emerged into the light from the end of the tunnel. They were lightly dressed in flannel shorts. There were twenty in all, each with a registration number on his breast.

Pierre clutched a stop watch. The vast crowd cheered. The starter loaded his gun for this first event, the one hundred metres. The runners broke up into three sections. The American Lane positioned himself at the starting line. He looked down along the track to the man holding the tape. Pierre and Marie watched nervously, both holding their breath.

"This is it at last", said Marie, kissing him.

Sloane lifted his hat. The gun went off. The runners bounded down the track, everyone watched with bated breath. Lane was the first to reach the tape. The crowds cheered, 'America! America!'. Pierre's stopwatch read twelve and one fifteenth of a second. As the runners took their place for the second heat Prince Constantine turned to Sloane.

"Ah, we have a young Greek runner, Kondylis, he's very fast."

"He'll have to watch out for Curtis, one of our chaps", replied Sloane.

"My gold's on the Greek", replied Constantine.

The gun was raised, a shot rang out. The crowd went wild with excitement, as Kondylis led the field. The Prince felt his side could win. But it was the American who crossed the finishing line.

"Not bad, twelve and a fifth seconds again," said Michael.

"The Americans are doing very well", observed Constantine.

"Don't worry, sir, there will be a few Greek winners. It's in your blood", replied Pierre.

The gun went off again, with the American Burke covered the distance in twelve seconds. The German Hoffman came second. The elated crowd waved the American flag.

"Three out of three, not bad!" said Sloane.

Two Greek youths stepped forward, bronzed and muscular, Persakis and Tufferi.

"Oh look, the triple jump is about to start. They look just like Greek Gods!" said Marie.

Pierre informed her that the American Connolly was taking part too. Persakis went first and jumped twelve point five metres. Then Tufferi jumped twelve point seven metres. Connolly took his position. There was a roar from the American supporters as Connolly bounded into the air, to a distance of thirteen point seven metres.

"It's amazing, the Americans are winning everything", said Constantine.

Men from the Greek Royal Navy hoisted the American flag at .the entrance to the stadium. Fourteen men took their positions, including the Australian Flack for the eight hundred metres race."There are no Greeks in this one", said Constantine.

"I'd put my money on Flack, he's very experienced. He's used to the dust of the outback", said Sloane.

The gun went off. Pierre picked up his opera glasses and followed Flack round the field. He eventually broke the tape, the crowd roared its approval. For the second heat of the eight hundred metres the Frenchman Lermisaux put on a pair of white gloves, and bowed to the King. He took his position.

"What is he doing with those damn stupid gloves?" asked Michael.

"He's a bit eccentric, old Lermisaux, but wearing the white gloves is his way of showing respect for the King", explained Pierre.

The gun went off and the Frenchman went bounding down the track proudly, followed by the very young Athenian Golemis.

"You can do it, boy! You can do it" exclaimed Constantine. The Frenchman beat the Athenian by inches.

"Your boys seem to have a bit of an edge on us Greeks", said Constantine dryly.

"We train harder, that's all", replied Sloane.

"The discus is next. If we don't win this, Ulysses will turn in his grave", said Constantine.

The sun was sinking in the sky. There were eleven participants in this next event: one Frenchman, one Swede, one American, one Englishman, three Danes, one German and three Greeks. For a moment, the crowd held their breath. The three Greeks entered the stadium, bronzed and muscular from prolonged exercise in the sun.

"They look as if they've stepped straight from legend", said

Marie.

"I'm beginning to understand why women spectators were banned from the Ancient Olympics," said Michael, laughing.

One after the other the contestants threw the discus until three remained: the two Greeks Versis, Anvopoulos and the American Garrett. Versis had the beauty of a Greek statue, winning the admiration of everyone. He stepped forward almost as if in slow motion and threw the bronze disc into the air. The crowd went wild with excitement. Anvopoulos threw next but did not reach the same distance. Michael turned to Sloane.

"What do you say, Sloane, do you think you have a chance?"

"I'm not sure. The discus is part of Greek tradition. It is like trying to teach Italians how to make spaghetti."

Garrett hurled the disc into the air. Everyone watched with bated breath as the disc struck the ground, raising the dust. Garrett had won! Connolly ran up and embraced him; the rest of the Americans lifted him into the air. Sloane got up and rushed down to Garrett.

"You've done it! You've beaten them at their own game!" he cried.

With this event the programme of the first day came to an end. The Royal Family departed amid enthusiastic cheering. The bands played the national anthem. The crowds emerged from the stadium and poured into the city. Huge festivities followed in the evening. The city seemed to float in shimmering light and music filled the air.

***

The Princeton Boys

Ellery Clarke

Thomas Curtis

CHAPTER SEVENTEEN

In the struggle of games he has won
The glory of his desire,
Whose hair is tied with thick garlands
For victory with his hands
Or swiftness of foot.
Men's valour is judged by their fates.

NEMIAN V

The Start 100 meters.

Prince Constantine on the sideline.

The Princeton Team

Herbert Jameson, Robert Garrett, Francis Lane, Albert Tyler

Sloane hosted a victory banquet for his team at the American Embassy. The noise of their celebrations washed over the Greek table nearby which held Averoff, Prince Constantine, Vikelas, Pierre, Marie, Michael and Helena. Pierre whispered to Michael that he wished they would be a little more discreet, in view of the fact that the Greeks had won nothing all day.

Pierre had observed the Americans basking in their glory. He sensed a certain resentment among the Greeks. They wanted victory too, but they could not even win at their own event, the discus.

Michael had wanted to talk to Helena all day since he had first seen her arriving at the stadium with her father Georgias Averoff. She had a face which reminded him of the classical proportions that the Greeks had captured in their finest statues. Her eyebrows were finely arched. Her lips curled towards the edge against her fine bones. Her flowing hair framed a beautifully oval face, adorned by gold earrings carved as dolphins.

Helena had noticed Michael too, but she never indulged in conversation with young men in the presence of her father. Michael saw his chance to speak with her.

"It's so beautiful in Greece. I feel myself falling under its spell every day, more and more. I wish I had the chance to see more of your country. I would like to stay on after the games. If only I had a guide ... would you help me, Helena?"

"Oh, Monsieur Breal, I'd like to, but I will have to ask my father."

Before he could enter into deeper discussion Pierre had risen to propose a toast to all his new found friends.

"Ladies and gentlemen, I would like to propose a toast to Greece; to the Greek people and to our gracious hosts; to Georgias

Averoff who made this all possible. Above all, to the Marathon. May the best man win!"

Everyone raised their glasses. Averoff looked at the guests, laughing and said:

" Best man! We don't care about that, what we want is a Greek. It's been over a thousand years since the Marathon was run and I would like to see a Greek win it. In fact, I'm prepared to offer a large sum of money to the winner, if he's a Greek!"

"But that's impossible; it would defeat the whole point of these Games with their amateur ethics. This cannot be about prize money", said Pierre, quite disturbed by Averoff's suggestion.

"But people are offering cattle, sheep, wine, even a lifetime of free haircuts to the winner. The Greek people want a Greek winner, a national hero. I don't see why I can't throw in some prize money. But wait! This is an idea which is better, more in the ancient tradition; you'll like it, Pierre. I am prepared to offer the hand in marriage of my daughter, Helena, to the Greek who wins the Marathon."

Some of the guests laughed, taking it as a joke. Michael and Marie were shocked and silent. Helena went white, jumped up and left the table. Michael followed. Averoff laughed, "Ah, a fit of girlish hysterics. Ignore her ... it will pass."

Everyone realised for the first time that there was another side to the character of the benefactor of the Games. The man who had believed in Pierre's idealism was now throwing his daughter like a dice in a lottery. This was a display of primitive chauvinism. Pierre whispered to the prince.

"Surely Averoff's not serious! It's a bit extreme, don't you think?"

"Perhaps," replied the Prince,"but for a girl as beautiful as I Helena I'd run the damn race myself."

Pierre said sadly, "I am amazed at how seriously the Greeks take their national pride. It saddens me. I never meant these Games to be about nationalism. The dream is to promote peace and co-operation. It's not about nationalism, sectarianism or racism ... we could do without all this."

"You have to be realistic, Pierre. You'll never get rid of those things. People are selfish, proud, and ignorant ... it's human nature", replied the Prince.

"But they are the very things that will destroy the Games, Your Highness, if we're not careful. I am sure the Games will continue and be watched around the world one day, but the ideal will be forgotten… "

"Pierre! Pierre! Cheer up, have another drink. This is no time to get depressed about the future of the Games. Think about the Marathon. Let's drink to that!"

***

Michael found Helena standing outside in tears on the balcony.

"Helena, are you all right?"

"I'm fine."

"Please, don't be upset. I'm sure your father didn't mean it," said Michael, offering her his handkerchief.

"You don't know my father. He does mean it. He's a good man in many ways, but he's living in the dark ages. As far as he's concerned I'm his property to dispose of as he pleases, just as if I was a sheep or an olive grove."

"You don't have to obey him."

"Oh Michael, where would I go, what else can I do? I can't disobey my father and stay under his roof ... you don't know Greece."

"I can't bear to stand by and watch you handed over as some sort of prize. I won't let it happen."

Helena returned to her room, consoled by Michael's words, but he could not change the course of events. He had promised to talk to Pierre who could, perhaps, influence her father's decision.

***

After the party Michael decided that he should speak to Pierre in his hotel room and explain the position. Pierre looked strangely worried. Michael had not seen him like this before.

Michael and Pierre continued their discussion late into the night. This latest incident left them dumbfounded. Pierre had envisaged problems, but this issue was beyond his comprehension.

It will be difficult to change his mind. I have already spoken to Averoff."

We cannot let her be in lieu of prize money! It's barbaric! If Greek wins the Marathon, I won't be there for the ceremony. Helena and I will be long gone!"

Leaving me to deal with the outraged father. Wonderful!" said Pierre smiling.

Exactly. What are friends for?"

"I'll talk to Averoff about the situation again," replied Pierre anxiously.

he dining room at the hotel was empty except for Averoff and Philemon who lingered over their brandy and cigars.

"I cannot believe that in the whole of Greece there isn't someone who can win this race for us", said Philemon despairingly.

Of course there is, we just have to find him", replied Averoff, with all the confidence of one who knows the power of money. All the same, it's easier said than done", commented Philemon. I don't care what it costs, I want to see a Greek win the Marathon. Do you think that's unforgivable?"

At that point an army officer, Major Papadopolous, approached them, dressed in traditional Greek uniform. Averoff did not waste time. Like all Greek tycoons of his generation, to him time and money were no obstacles. Averoff, having signed the cheque, was now orchestrating events.

The major joined them and bowed formally to Averoff, who addressed him as"Major Papa".

"We've got a problem. We need a runner. Do you know any?""Afraid not, sir", said the major respectfully.

"Do you mean to tell me that in the whole damn army you can not find one man who can run! hmm? No wonder the country is in such a state!"

"Actually, sir, there is someone. There is a young man who served under me a few years ago. He can run like the wind.

What is his name?... Loues, Spiridon Loues!... never seen anything like it."

"Now you're talking! That's the stuff! So where is he? Runs like the wind you say… perfect!"

"He left the army a few years ago and went back to the mountains. He's a shepherd. Let me see… he's from Maroussi, that's it."

"I don't care how you do it, Major, but I want this man found. It's a matter of national importance, do you understand me?" exclaimed Averoff.

"Yes, Sir, I shall do my best."

"I should hope so. The pride of all Greece depends on this race", said Averoff, puffing on his cigar.
***

Papa's mission seemed to be ordained by royal decree. He planned to travel to the village of Maroussi immediately. He set off before dawn on horseback. He galloped along the streets of Athens. Papa made his way to a dirt track which would take him to his destination. It was a long winding road heading south. His horse kicked up dust as he tried to negotiate the rough terrain.

After two hours he reached the edge of the village, which was made up of small whitewashed houses. A shepherd told him that Loues was up in the hills but would soon come down. He pointed the way to the taverna, where he knew Loues's father would be. There he found an old man with a white beard, sitting in the shade drinking ouzo. This was Loues's father Eumaeus.

Papa explained the purpose of his mission."It's a long way to Marathon," Eumaeus said."But Spiridon will do his best for Greece," replied Papa.

"I do not understand .... we sit in the taverna, you come and tell me about the race at Marathon. My son he looks after sheep, but you say he has to run for Greece Why? If he goes, there is no one to look after the sheep I am too old now," said Eumaeus in great distress.

"Do not worry, my friend, I will see that your sheep are looked after," replied Major Papa.
"But Papa, I do not know this race is too long and too dangerous the Greek sun is too hot."

As the two men continued talking, they were unaware that Loues had arrived in the village with his sheep. He was muscular and tanned from the endless days under the hot Greek sun. He wore cotton trousers, tied with string around the waist, and a loose cotton shirt that billowed in the breeze.

Loues's figure blocked the doorway and the two men looked up. Papa observed his jet black hair and his steely blue eyes, which were clear and alert.

"0h, Spiridon, you're back Major Papa has come all the way from Athens to find you. He has been sent by Georgias Averoff, the richest man in Greece they want you to run in the Marathon."

"The Marathon, what is this Marathon?" replied Spiridon, taking a seat and pouring himself a cup of goat's milk.

"Yes, the Marathon," replied Major Papa."A run from Marathon to Athens is twenty six miles. We need tough runners like you to run for Greece."

"But why me?" questioned Spiridon.

"Because I remember you as one of the best long distance runners in Greece… the Americans have won all the medals at the games… we need a Greek to win."

"If a Greek does not win," said Papa, "our people will be sad. The King will be angry."

"I don't know," replied Spiridon.

"I am just doing my duty… a Greek winning the Marathon will bring back national pride, we need a great victory. There are many prizes for the winner: money, food, land," said Papa anxiously.

"Spiridon has to carry water up the mountains every day and look after the goats and sheep, to make a few drachmas ... it could be a great opportunity, Spiridon," said his father looking into his eyes.

Spiridon got up from his seat and walked towards the door. He looked out across the landscape. This was the place he had lived and worked in all his life. He had never been to Athens. He had lived a quiet life among simple peasants. This opportunity could change everything for him and his family and take them out of poverty. The decision was not difficult: he would take part in the Marathon.

***

They sat that evening and looked out upon the bronzed mountains of Greece, stretching off into the distance. The intense white light of the Greek sun began to fade across the parched landscape. Athens was far off in the distance, its skyline melting in the shimmering light. Shepherds and their flocks made their way along an ancient beaten track, winding its way up among the mountains. Ahead of them was a large group of sheep and goats.

"Look there! Who are those men?" asked Papa.

"They travel far from their homes for most of the year. They go in search of work," replied Eumaeus, "to feed the children and look after their parents."

"It must be very hard for them."

"It is a difficult life, an endless journey. We have been shepherding these mountains for centuries. We may be poor, but we are not poor in spirit. We have our past, our beliefs. My father called me Eumaeus, after the shepherd who was faithful to Ulysses after his wanderings home from Troy. He was a good faithful shepherd who did not forget Ulysses.

Ulysses's wife Penelope was being hounded by suitors who wished to marry her, men who had once been loyal to Ulysses. There is a message in this story. It is about strength of love and loyalty to one's friends. Ulysses had spent twenty years on his journey home from Troy. All the other men who had travelled with him around the shores of the Mediterranean had met their death. But when Ulysses was washed up upon the shore in rags he sought the help of a shepherd named Eumaeus who brought him back to his palace.

There he met his faithful dog Argos, who greeted him after

waiting for his master for twenty years. Then Argos rolled over and died. There Ulysses was able to claim his palace, his kingdom and his wife. The faith that his shepherd had is the greatest power of the soul."

Eumaeus looked at Spiridon. He picked up a bowl of milk, drank some and then looked out upon the landscape of faded yellows. His thoughts traced back in time.

In 490 BC. an Athenian soldier who had won many prizes at the ancient Olympic Games was in Athens. Pheidippides was his name. News came that the Persians were about to land on .Greek soil at Marathon. He travelled for two days and two nights to seek aid from the Spartans. The Spartans refused to help, as it was on the eve of a religious festival. His mission having failed, he returned to fight the great battle of Marathon.

Soon the Greeks defeated the Persians at Marathon. Someone would have to tell the elders in Athens. Pheidippides was chosen. So he set off from the plains of Marathon. He ran up through the hills, but as he ran onwards the sun began to rise and its intense heat beat down on him. After several hours of running Pheidippides reached the edge of Athens and he could see the Acropolis, high above the city.

People realised that he was one of the soldiers who had gone to fight at Marathon, as he ran along the city's streets. They stopped in their tracks as he ran past them. When he reached the city square he became surrounded by Athenian men, women and children, and some of the elder folk. Pheidippides cried out, 'Rejoice, we have conquered' and dropped dead.

Eumaeus looked at his son and placed his hand on his shoulder.

"Pheidippides was not just a soldier, he was a victor of many of the prizes in the Olympic Games, and for him running was a pursuit of excellence, of the mind and the body. You must never forget that." Eumaeus passed Spiridon the bowl of milk and looked out upon the landscape.

***

Papa stayed for the evening service at the village church which was thronged with the local people, as it was just after Easter. They sang joyfully, and when the music finished the priest motioned to them to lift their candles. He then lit the large Pascal candle. Eumaeus whispered to Papa,
"The holy flame of the Resurrection!"

***

Marathon Battle

Athena, Goddess of peace and defensive war

Ulyesses returns to Itkica to claim the hand of his lost wife Peŋelope, killing all her suitors.

CHAPTER EIGHTEEN

MARATHON 1896

For if any man delights in expense and effort
And sets in action high gifts shaped by the Gods,
And with him his destiny
Plants the glory which he desires,
Already he casts his anchor on the furthest
edge of bliss,
And the Gods honour him.

ISTHMIAN VI
ATHENS

The start of the first marathon of modern times. It was Michael Breal, a French student of classics at the Sorbonne who suggested the idea to De Coubertin.

Before the Marathon race
by Castaigne

100,000 people waited for the marathon winner
Loues, winner of the marathon. A Picture published widely in the Greek press.

100,000 people waited for the Marathon winner.

March 30th, 1896. 1.30pm. Athens was empty. The stadium was packed to capacity. Pierre looked down Kiffisia Avenue. He could see the banks of the river Illisus, where Socrates had once strolled with the playful Phaedrus. It seemed as if everyone had traced a single pathway to Athens. The streets were like a vast floating wheatfield.

This was the race that everyone had waited for: the Marathon. It was believed that no-one could complete the course in under three hours. For those three hours everyone in the stadium would rely on wild rumour. The occasional announcement of a name would give them an idea of how the race was going.

Many contestants had pulled out of the race the evening before. There was a certain amount of friendly rivalry among the athletes. They discussed the strategy for the race. There was a superstition among them that perhaps none of them would complete the distance.

Among the Greek entrants there was added pressure to win. Prayers were offered in thousands of churches throughout Greece. Men, women and children were lighting candles all over the land. It was the prospect of the Marathon being run again which excited the Greek imagination. The Marathon had raised the Games to the status of something sacred. Yet there was also the fear that the competitors might die through exhaustion.

Apprehension had mounted as the day dawned. How could this race be run in the heat and the dust, over the difficult terrain, for forty two kilometres? No-one had trained for the course. The twenty five contestants would begin their run at 2 o'clock in the afternoon. It would be a most memorable contest. Even the starting gun of General Papa would become a relic after the event was over.

***

At the Palace Averoff, Constantine & Pierre greeted each runner. Averoff turned to Pierre as Loues lined up.

"This is Spiridon Loues, our great hope for a Greek winner".

"I am proud to be here".

"Well, I wish you well; this is Pierre De Coubertin, the founder of the Games".

"I am honoured to meet you", said Pierre.

"Thank you, I will do my best for Greece".

"Run with the Gods", said Pierre smiling at him.

"I can feel the wind beneath my wings", replied Loues, shaking hands with Pierre.

***

In the Stadium enclosure Pierre and Marie sat talking.

"I am very worried about Helena, Pierre; I can understand why she refused to come today."

"Michael wouldn't come either."

"What do you expect? They're madly in love."

Averoff came to their table, cigar in hand.

"Pierre… Marie… good to see you."

Marie turned away to look across the countryside.

"Is something the matter? Is it something I've said?"

"Yes, it is actually. I think your offering Helena as a prize is unforgivable."

"What do you mean, Marie? Every girl in Greece is going to want to marry the winner of the Marathon."

" Not if she's in love with another man."

"In love! My daughter in love with another man! Who is it anyway?"

"Michael Breal, and he loves her too." Averoff paused, puffing on his cigar.

"That is very unfortunate. But you must understand my position. I cannot go back on my word. My honour is at stake. The winner of the Marathon is expecting to claim Helena as his prize. I cannot retract my offer."

***

Loues was silent and alone in the church at Marathon. He knelt at the altar which was filled with rows of candles, illuminating ,the statue of the Virgin. He whispered a prayer. He crossed himself beneath the great Greek Byzantine chandeliers and the frescoed dome.

MARATHON

Twenty five runners lined up on the bridge at Marathon. The most noticeable was Lermisaux. He insisted again on wearing fine white calf gloves. He wore them as a mark of respect to the King.

The runners took their places at the starting position. The intense heat of midday still lingered to this hour. It would remain high and hot until at least half past three.

In the village was a row of twenty soldiers in Greek uniform. They held their trumpets by their sides. To the right of them were another twenty five soldiers standing beside their horses. Stable hands milled about, fixing their stirrups and attaching the national flag to each of the horses. The women moved around and handed out drinks, while the children played. In the shadows hundreds of old men and women sat dressed in black.

The church bells of Marathon began to ring and the twenty five contestants marched into the square. A large number of spectators gathered to see them off. The foot soldiers lifted their trumpets to the sound of the bugle call. The runners stepped forward to the starting line and the Major loaded his gun.

"This race from Marathon to Athens has not been run for over one thousand years. It was a Greek soldier who last ran this distance, when we Greeks defeated our enemy. He ran to Athens to tell of a great victory. I hope that you all run this race today in the same spirit. God speed to you all!" announced Major Papa.

The gun went off. The race had started. The runners disappeared from view out of the village; and the villagers threw flowers after them. The soldiers on horseback followed immediately after.

As the race began, the runners broke quickly and by half a kilometre Lermisaux had gone forward to lead the field. He sped towards the village of Pikerni, along a slope. The news from Pikerni went on ahead. It was sent by soldiers on horseback in relay, located along the Marathon route into Athens.

The runners were followed by mounted soldiers, each with a second on horseback.

Lermisaux led the field. After him was the Australian Flack; the American Blake; the Hungarian Kellener, and then the, Greeks Lavrenti, Vasilakos and Loues heading across the plains of Marathon. The Major galloped up ahead of Lermisaux and led the way. Villagers lined the route, throwing flowers and shouting,"Marathon! Marathon!" The runners reached a ridge and two of the contestants lost their balance and fell to the ground. Some of the horses careered off the track and the soldiers tried to calm them.

Each time rumours spread from one village to another. By Pikerni there was a clear report. In the stadium the word spread.

The crowd sighed with small gasps of disappointment: the Greek runners were well behind. Lermisaux had run to Pikerni, fifteen kilometres distant from Marathon, in fifty two minutes. He had a lead of three kilometres over Flack who was second. He was followed by Blake and Kellener. Flack had narrowly beaten Blake in the fifteen hundred metres on the second day. Again these tall powerfully built men were doing battle.

Some time later Papa accused one of the athletes of swallowing from a bottle of brandy. Blake's shoes were beginning to tear to shreds. Lavrenti and Loues, childhood rivals from the village of Maroussi, were engaged in mortal running combat.

As the midday sun beat down the runners began to sweat heavily. They passed through the village of Pikerni. There were many tables lined with food and drink, which the runners grabbed as they passed. They threw their empty glasses to the ground. Papa dropped back to Blake.

"Who's in the lead?" asked Blake.

"Lermisaux," replied Papa.

"I don't believe it! The Frenchie with the gloves," replied Blake, amazed, panting for breath.

Loues was still at the rear, pacing himself, when his second shouted at him "Run, run, run!"

The sun began to lose its intensity. For the runners it made no difference, for inside their blood was already boiling; it was as if flames were coming from within. To Pikerni the course had been downward. Now they would wind upwards, climbing beyond the sea level over the next ten kilometres, running towards the sun. Their bodies felt the strain. Their muscles became cramped, coiled so taut that it was painful. The weariness started to enter their lungs and legs. Their heads had no weight, and their bodies lost sensation.

Lermisaux knew from his second that Blake the American was approaching. He accelerated up the hill in long powerful strides. He called now on all his physical resources.

They reached the village of Lavati. Lermisaux was followed by Blake. They ran under the triumphal arch which was decked with flowers. Loues was now being followed by some peasants from the village, who ran with him as a kind of guard of honour. Suddenly he began to pick up speed. Papas galloped ahead, kicking up dust as he passed Lermisaux who staggered and fell: et he quickly climbed up again and raced on.

***

At the rear of the race was Vasilakos. He came to a winding road near one of the mountain ridges, where a carriage was parked nearby. He quickly jumped into the carriage and took off at great speed up one of the back roads. He was spotted by Lavrenti who looked on disgusted and screamed,"You cheat, Vasilakos, you stinking cheat!"

Vasilakos lay back in the carriage, covered in dust and exhausted. With him was a friend from his village, Costas.

"I thought I was going to die back there," panted Vasilakos.

"Do not worry, my friend, have some wine; we have plenty of time to get to Athens, for you to win this race."

"No, no problem. Who is winning?" asked Vasilakos.

"The Frenchie in white gloves, but not for long! I will let you out one kilometre before Athens. Remember, today it won't just a great victory for Greece, it will be for us."

Lermisaux continued to lead the field. The road had become much rougher with rocky outcrops. A Greek runner, his feet covered with blood, staggered and fell into the dust. His second up next to him, trying to restrain his mount. The Greek over in the sun, while a doctor and nurse rushed to his side. They placed him on a stretcher and carried him into a wagon.

***

A messenger arrived at the stadium and rushed to the royal enclosure where everyone was waiting anxiously for news.

"Who is winning, my friend?" asked Averoff.

"The Frenchman, he's leading all the way," replied the

messenger.

"Thank God!" cried Helena, kissing Michael.

"How's my boy Blake getting on?" asked Sloane.

"He's collapsed, he's out I'm afraid; Flack is second."

"I don't believe it," replied Sloane.

"But where is Loues? Where is Loues?" questioned Averoff.

"He's at the rear," said the messenger.

"It's a disgrace. He's supposed to be the fastest man in Greece," said Averoff.

"How much longer will we have to wait!" said the Prince impatiently.

"I cannot say, my Lord - maybe one more hour."

***

Loues continued to be joined by runners from the villages he passed through. Blake caught up with Lermisaux. Then there was a bitter battle for the lead. Lermisaux sprinted ahead at a desperate pace, sweat pouring from his face. He reached another ridge and began to climb the hill. He struggled to the top of the ridge, followed by his second on horseback, then staggered and became delirious as the sun beat down on him.

As Lermisaux was given a laurel by a girl, his legs began to wobble. A new sharp incline made him crash behind his second. His body reduced almost to pulp. His daring effort to lead from start to finish had failed. He lay crumpled on the ground, surrounded by a wreath and his tattered white gloves. He was filthy from the dust of the course, which covered his two completely limp and lifeless hands. Blake immediately went into the lead.

But Lermisaux rose again. He rose as if from the dead. The little figure of the Frenchman got up from the ground. He ran a little until the thirty-two kilometre mark. At Agia Paraskevi he fell for the second time, bruised and worn. The gloves were still on his hands.

Lermisaux then collapsed for the final time. The Frenchman was carried to the medical wagon. Now Blake was leading the field. He arrived at the next village. He saw villagers waving the Greek and American flags. His second kept right beside him, shouting encouragement.

"How far now?" Blake asked his second.

"About ten kilometres."

"I can't take much more of this!"

"You can do it," said his second, willing him on.

***

Vasilakos was still in the carriage with Costas. Costas saw that his friend had had too much to drink and slapped his face. The carriage came to a grinding halt at a bend, spewing up dust.

Costas spoke. "We are getting near to Athens. It is time for you to get out. But, my friend, I think you've drunk too much wine, pull yourself together. Make sure you bring that gold cup back to the village. If you do, you'll become the richest man in

Greece," said Costas, trying to sober him up.

Vasilakos stumbled from the carriage and rejoined the runners at the rear. Fresh and well rested, he sprinted up past Loues and on towards Blake who was still leading. He sprinted ahead at an extraordinary speed. The rest of the runners tried desperately to keep up with him, Blake struggling furiously to maintain his position.

"Oh my God! Where did he come from?" cried Blake, amazed at the sudden appearance of Vasilakos.

Blake was numb. He had no longer an even stride. His will alone kept him going. His second urged him on. The climb from Pikerni became steeper. It had claimed its first victim.

Blake's lungs were bursting. He ran as if the pride of all America depended on him. Vasilakos sped ahead with a spiteful grin on his face. Blake's feet started to bleed on the rough surface of the road. He threw his arms into the air and screamed"America! America!"

His second watched in disbelief. The Harvard man crumpled on to the side of the road. His whole body was bathed in blood. Every pore was crying in despair. The laces of his shoes stuck to his bleeding feet. Blake was out of the race!

His second jumped off his horse and tried to revive him. Blake was carried into a taverna and laid on a makeshift table. He was in intense pain. The Greek doctor looked at his severely cut feet. A nurse tried to stem the flow of blood.

"This is madness… the Marathon should be stopped!" said the doctor, sickened by the sight of Blake.

***

In the stadium, at the royal box, a soldier dismounted. He carried a letter from General Papa to the King. The King read it and turned to Averoff.

"It's from Major Papa. Many of the runners have collapsed and are badly injured."

"Perhaps we should call the race off. Maybe it can't be run; maybe it never existed," said the King.

"You can't stop the race. It can be run," said Michael, listening intently.

"What if these men die?" said the King.

"If you stop the race it will destroy the Games," said Michael emphatically.

"It's a great symbol," said Pierre.

"I think Michael is right," said Constantine.

The King thought for a moment, consulted with one of his aides, and then nodded his approval to continue.

***

Vasilakos, now leading, approached his own village. His friends and relatives jumped for joy at seeing their favourite winning the race. The women threw flowers at him.

"Vasilakos! Vasilakos! Our hero!" cried the villagers.

"Vasilakos, I love you, I love you!" cried another, as she threw her arms around him and held on to him like a woman possessed. As Vasilakos tried to shake her off they both crashed into a table, laden with food and wine. Vasilakos was injured, and was now out of the race.

***

At Chilandri, nine kilometres from Athens, Flack who had taken the lead was challenged by Spiridon Loues. No-one had noticed the slow steady pace of Loues. He had come up alongside Flack at the village of Chilandri. For four kilometres they kept within fifty strides of each other. Their feet were vibrating, their lips trembling, knees shaking. Pain tested their willpower.

Flack sped through another village, gulping some wine as flowers were thrown in his path. Papa appeared beside him.

"How far is Athens?" asked Flack.

"About six kilometres," replied Papa.

"Bloody hell, this is worse than the outback!" said Flack, collapsing slowly to the ground. Papa stopped, dismounted and ran to his side, trying to help him to his feet, but Flack just stared up at the sun.

"No, no, I can't go on! This is too much for one man to take." finally Flack rose and ran on. Loues increased his tempo. Flack could not believe it; he had passed him. How was it possible? Then, with a spurt, Loues went far ahead. Flack felt a wrenching movement in his back. The pain had gone through him. He could control his body no further. He fell in the dust. He seemed to hear the sound of thunder. There was a rumbling and blankness in his mind. He lay unconscious on the ground.

Meanwhile Loues raced ahead. Within minutes he was far ahead of the field. The Acropolis came into view. Loues passed the school at Rizarios. One of the villagers fired a gunshot into the air. Hundreds of people gathered and shouted,"0 Nikitis. 0 Nikitis !" Papa galloped up to Loues.

"Keep going, my boy, you'll make us all proud. You must win now. Victory is assured!" shouted Papa. Loues remembered Pierrer's parting words,"Run with the Gods!"

"I must go and tell the King!" cried Papa as he galloped off at full speed towards the stadium.

A deathly silence hung over the crowd. Everyone sensed that something was about to happen. Papa appeared at the entrance to the stadium. He galloped up along the track, dismounted quickly and climbed the steps up to the king.

"I bring good news - it's a Greek, your Majesty, a Greek - Loues is winning!" said Papa with tears in his eyes.

The remaining runners were on the outskirts of Athens. It was as if the whole stadium was listening. The King was ecstatic. The Crown Princes jumped up from the review stand."Eleen! Eleen! A Greek! A Greek!" The stadium exploded with the sound of a cannon booming across Athens. What was happening? A Greek! A Greek! Can it be? It was what everyone hoped for. Even the foreigners were shouting the words"Eleen! Eleen!" Who was it? Everyone rose to their feet. When would the winner enter the stadium? How could anyone have run from Marathon to Athens? He was not only a victor, but a survivor.

Helena burst into tears. She ran out of the box with Michael in pursuit. The news spread like wildfire. An immense cry emerged from the crowd. The gunshot announcing the arrival of the Greek victor was heard. The King looked up."That's the signal.

He's arrived in Athens," said the King, his voice filled with emotion.

***

Down through the streets of Athens came the figure of Spiridon Loues. He had never come to Athens before. He had never left the village of Maroussi before. The heat of tile road had been intense. Yet he continued to stride. He gathered his strength, running along those great boulevards. In front of him he saw the enormous crowds, a swelling sea. All were waving the blue and white flag of Greece.

The spectators were now standing on their seats. Their eyes were glued to the entrance. Suddenly Loues appeared. He was sunburnt and covered in sweat and dust. The crowd roared"Eleen! Eleen! It's a Greek! It's a Greek!"

Everyone exploded with excitement. The cries echoed inside the stadium. The band played the national hymn. The arena was a frenzy of sounds. A delirium of emotion moved like a wave towards him.

Constantine jumped out of the royal box, followed by Prince George, to join Loues in the last lap.

"Loues! You have saved Greece! You have saved the Games!" cried Constantine.

Loues, too exhausted to speak, smiled. He nodded his head. Inside he was burning. His head was bigger than his whole body. Everything was racing in his mind. He was accompanied by two immense men, the Crown Princes of Greece running beside him. Hats were thrown in the air. Women threw their jewellery down on to the track. The words"A Greek! A Greek!" were heard, and in Greek,"0 Nikitis! 0 Nikitis! Long live the victor," echoed throughout the stadium.

For a brief moment he felt that Nike the winged goddess of victory had descended from the heavens to greet him. He could feel the wind beneath her wings. Like in ancient Greece, in reaching the finishing line he had become immortal.

Loues crossed the finishing line marked by statues of Zeus on both sides. He couldn't see. His eyes were blind with disbelief. He was lifted into the air. He was carried by the Princes to where the King sat. The King rose and threw his hat upwards. Loues approached him. He saw the royal tears as the King chanted with closed eyes,"Eleen! Eleen! A Greek! A Greek!"

The Greek flag was raised. The crowd reached a feverish pitch of frenzy. Hats were thrown into the air. The gunners fired several rounds in quick succession. Thousands of pigeons and doves were launched into the sky. Everyone waved handkerchiefs and flags. Olive branches and wreaths were thrown on the track. The crowds roared and the bands continued to play the national anthem of Greece.

"This moment is sacred," said King George, throwing his arms around Loues and kissing his forehead.

"A glorious victory, my son, a glorious victory," said the King. Everyone in the royal box shook Loues's hand and threw their arms around him.

"You have recreated history today," said Pierre, shaking Loues's hand.

The King opened the box with the sacred cup of Olympia. Loues knelt at his feet.

"Stand up, my son, we are your servants," said the King, placing the laurel wreath on his head. Then he lifted the cup for the crowd to see.

"This is the sacred cup of Olympia; my forefathers lit the sacred flame of Olympia with oil from this cup. We honour the victor of the Marathon with this great symbol."

Loues took the cup and kissed it. Then Averoff turned to Loues."And now, I have the honour of offering you my daughter's hand in marriage.

Loues paused for a moment with a faint smile on his lips.

"Thank you, sir. But I have a wife already," replied Loues. Marie turned to Pierre with a sense of astonishment.

Then they hurried out of the royal box to tell Helena and Michael the wonderful news. The two Crown Princes lifted Loues once more into the air and the band played on.

***

Loues joined in the last lap by Prince Constantine of Greece

Loues is greeted by King George

Loues carrying a Greek flagleading the Victory ceremony of the Marathon

Loues - The Victory Parade

Loues receives his Olympic medal and diploma

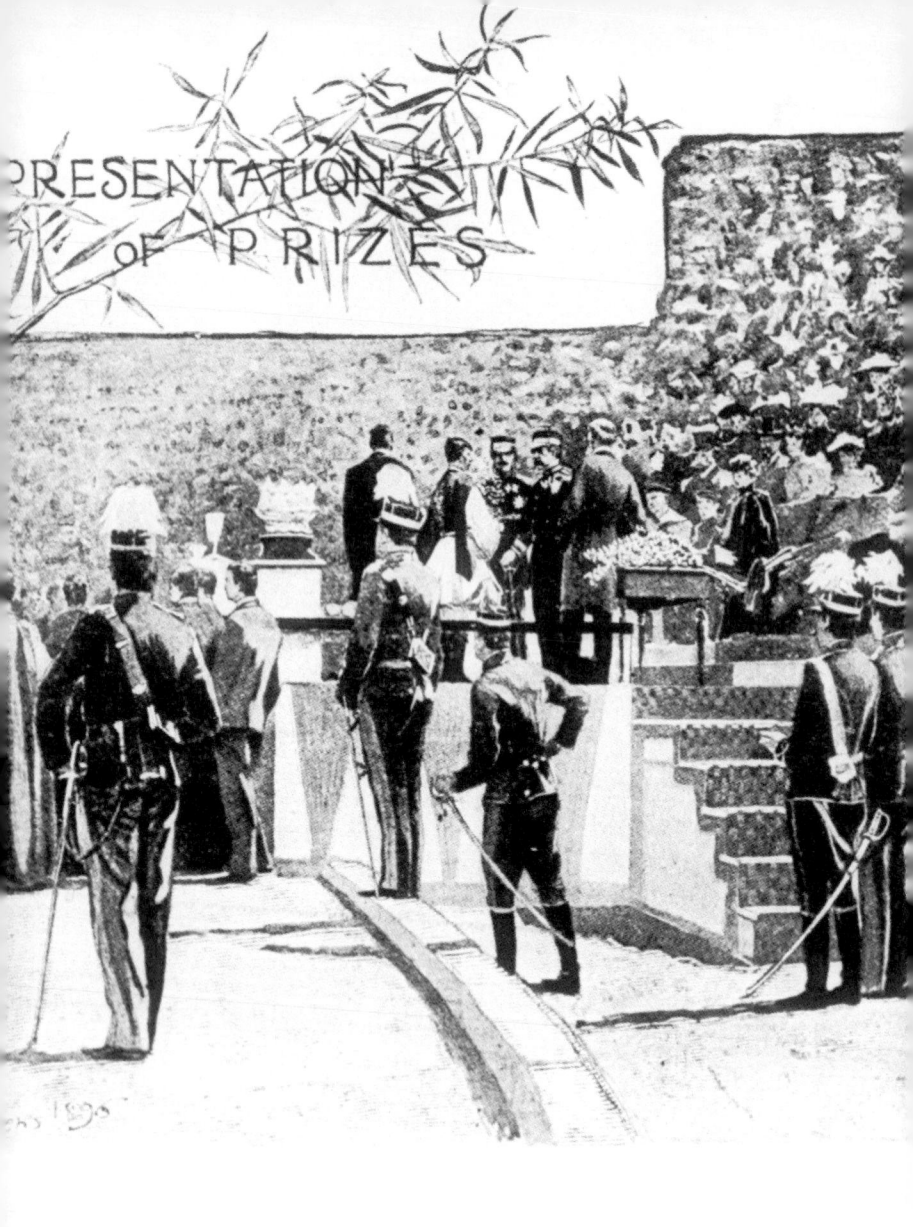

Loues presented with his prize by the king of Greece

Loues seated with the American team,
Crown Prince Constantine, Prince George and Prince Nicholas.

CHAPTER NINETEEN

*Now keep the bow on the mark.
Come, my heart, at whom do we aim
And shoot from a gentle heart our shafts of glory?*

OLYMPIAN II

The Princeton Team, Lane, Jameson, Tyler, Garrett.

340

William Hoyt of Harvard and the Boston Athletic Association,
Winner of the pole vault

Albert Tyler, Princeton University

The Boston Team return home, to a heroes welcome.
Blake, Curtis, Clarke, Hoyt and Burke

Sophia Schliemann, wife of Heinrich, the man who discovered Troy, met with the American team and bid them farewell.

The next day the King paid tribute to the champions at a great breakfast party. It was attended by members of the International Committee, the Greek Hellenic Association and the various competitors. In all there were two hundred and sixty guests.

At 10 o'clock the King entered in admiral's uniform. The Philharmonic Society of Corfu played the national hymn. Then three cantatas of Samaras were played. The King was saluted by the long lines of guests. He took his place at the centre of the table laden with flowers, wine and fruit. Prince George sat to his right with Prince Nicholas to his left.

Pierre was greeted by an unexpected guest, by Sophia Schliemann. She had been the wife of Heinrich Schliemann who had discovered Troy. Schliemann was now dead. Now a respected friend of Greece, on his tomb the words "Schliemann the hero" had been inscribed. Memories of Pierre's boyhood flooded back to him, memories of Troy and a burning city.

Sophia smiled at him sweetly and congratulated him on his great achievement. She looked like an ancient Greek Princess and wore beaten gold jewellery. Here was the woman who had seen the walls of Troy!

The King received Loues and his father.
"It is an honour to meet the father of such a fine young man, a national hero," said the King.

"I am proud, I am proud. You must come and visit us in our village one day. We have good food and good wine there," replied Loues's father, honoured to be greeted by the King.

"I would be happy to do that," said the King.

At the end of the banquet the King rose and gave the following toast:

"Permit me, gentlemen, to express to you the pleasure we have all felt, on seeing you come to Greece in order to take part in the Olympic Games. With the warm welcome the people have given you, you have been able to judge for yourselves with what joy the Hellenic nation has received you. I therefore seize this opportunity to tender my warmest congratulations to those gentlemen who have been victorious in the competitions. I thank you all for coming here.

In a few days you will bid us farewell to return home. I wish you all good luck and God speed. I beg you to keep us in good remembrance and I hope you may never forget the emotions you shared with us, when the victor of the Marathon race entered the stadium. I am sorry that the Queen is ill and cannot be here, to her great regret; she wished me to bid you welcome in her name. Gentlemen, I drink to your health, in thanking you again and most sincerely for having come to Athens for the inaugural Olympic Games."

The King's toast was greeted with loud applause; Pierre was touched by the heroic speech. After waiting some moments until silence was restored, the King raised his glass and proposed another toast.

"Gentlemen, the re-establishment of the Olympic Games in the land of their classical birth has been crowned with complete and unexpected success. I am therefore delighted to be able to congratulate and thank you all today, all of you who have contributed or helped in bringing such results. I must express the gratitude of my nation, as well as my own, to the great benefactor of this country, Georgias Averoff, who has shown himself worthy to be classed with Herodius Atticus. On leaving Greece our foreign guests will be able to testify to the progress of this country. This has enabled us to work successfully in so short a time for a worthy inauguration of the Games.

Greece, who has been the mother and nurse of the Olympic Games in ancient times, and has undertaken to celebrate them once more today, can now hope, as their success has gone beyond all expectation, that the foreigners who have honoured her with their presence will remember Athens as the peaceful meeting place of all the nations, as the tranquil permanent seat of the Olympic Games. With that wish I drink, gentlemen, to the health of all those who have contributed to the success of the first modern Olympiad."

This speech was heartily applauded. Pierre noted, however, that the King spoke of a permanent place for the Games. He himself felt that they should not remain in Greece. For Pierre, the Games were truly an international affair and should be held in turn in various host countries. By the Games remaining in Greece they would become prey to nationalism. He had already seen proof of it. This would destroy the ideal.

But for the audience present this issue was overlooked in their enthusiasm. Philemon rose and gave an eloquent speech. It touched all present, and especially the King.

"The diamonds which have fallen from your lips, 0 King, glitter with such a lustre that even the most persuasive eloquence is outdone. Our sincerity and enthusiasm must make up for our eloquence. You have shown, Your Majesty, that you understand the high importance of the Grand Title of the Bear. You are King of the Hellenes, not only of those living free on the soil of Greece, but also those living in the unredeemed provinces and of those scattered about in different parts of the world. I render thanks to God who has granted that I have seen this beautiful festival, before I close my eyes forever."

Philemon's speech was filled with emotion and brought the audience to a state of elation. But it was Monsieur Hugo le Roux's speech that had the most profound message. The words of the journalist from Le Figaro touched Pierre.

"Sire, it is not only for those connected with me by ties of blood and race that I ask permission to raise my glass. It is for us all whom you have invited here and made welcome. We all have brought with us this wish in coming to Greece. Might only one of us be the winner of the Marathon Cup! But even when we saw approaching at the entrance of the stadium this peasant, there was none of us, whatever our nationality, who did not join in the general outburst of enthusiasm. We all felt as if Greek soil had run under the feet of her son to help him on to victory. It was to be a Greek who would come and say, 'Forget what divides you; barbarians are repulsed, civilisation triumphs for the second time.' In that moment, when your two sons of Greece led this child of Greece up to your throne, there were no more foreigners present in the stadium, neither were there any Greeks: we were all your subjects."

***

The golden evening light that summer brings bathed all of Athens. That evening a procession was held after the Games, where thousands of people gathered in Athens Avenue holding torches. As the light faded the flames became brighter. The procession was led by soldiers on horseback. The bands began playing at nine o'clock as the procession began. They were joined by thousands of students carrying multi-coloured Venetian lanterns. Then came the sailors, dressed in white, with civilians and members of the guard of Athens. The whole avenue was lit up by a river of fire that stretched off into the distance.

With a bugle call, the vast crowd of people moved forward like a stream of lava, pouring into Athens. The guards of the Olympic stadium paraded in red tunics and white helmets and bore the flags of all countries who took part in the Games. The endless procession entered Stadium Street, illuminating the arches that extended into the distance, framing this shimmering river of fire. The procession proceeded, to the sounds of the bands, to Constitution Square and the Palace.

There the whole of the royal family admired the sight from the balcony. King George and Constantine saluted the crowds. For Pierre, it was a moment he would not forget. It was the King of Greece who had once sent Dr. Brooke the cup; now he stood there on the balcony savouring the fruits of his idea. If only Dr. Brooke were alive to see this day, mused Pierre.

Pierre noted with sadness that the Games were not publicised in the British press. The British had not taken part. Their few athletes who entered did so individually. It was paradoxical that the Games, inspired by the English, were not supported by them. He could trace the reason back to Lord Ampthill's aristocratic elitism. He claimed that it was only the Anglo-Saxons who knew what sport was about.

***

As for the Americans, they returned home triumphant. News of their victories was announced in the New York and Boston newspapers. Pierre read of their return when he reached Paris, where he received many letters of congratulation.

The Bostonians made their way back via Rome, Paris and on to Bremen in Germany. In New York, on May 7th, 1896, a band greeted them with the tune 'See the Conquering Heroes Come.' Garret and his team were greeted by thousands of students from Princeton. The Olympic victors were carried on the shoulders of their cheering admirers. A great bonfire was lit and bells rang continuously. They were taken by the crowds to the Knickerbocker Club in Manhattan. A wave of emotion arose in the crowds. Later the victors were carried to an official reception in Fanueil Hall. They had won against great odds. They had inspired America, and their victory was a memorable one.

***

Connolly's career after the games was equally colourful. He never returned to Harvard. He became a member of the 9th Massachusetts Regiment of the U.S. Volunteers during the Spanish American Civil War. He was in the navy, and was engaged in the Battle of Santiago.

Drawing on his experiences at sea, he wrote a series of novels including"The Deep Sea's Toll", and"The Crested Seas". He also wrote a book about the Athens Games. His confrontation with his Dean at Harvard did not affect his successful career in journalism and as a novelist. On September 28th, 1901 he married Elizabeth Francis Hurley and settled in Dorchester, Massachusetts.

***

As for Garrett, he joined the banking house of his great grandfather and became President of the Provident Savings Bank and the Western National Bank. On his return to America he helped set up athletic contests and a gymnasium at Princeton, investing his own funds for the cause. In 1907 he married Katherine Barkett and had two children.

In 1908 he sought entry into the Maryland House of Representatives. He became owner of a newspaper, the Baltimore Country Union, and an illustrious collector of medieval and oriental manuscripts. In 1899 he went on an archaeological dig in Syria and wrote about his adventures.

***

Loues became the hero of the Athens Games. He returned to his native village where a legend grew around him. This twenty five year old Greek shepherd had taken Athens by storm when he ran into the ancient stadium. He became a national hero, known throughout Greece. Loues was showered with gifts, a lifetime of free wine, a million drachmas, and land. He disappeared from Athens, and was never seen there again until the Berlin Games.

***

Thomas Curtis, Boston Athletics Association, winner of the 100 metres

Souvenir poster of the Athens Games, 776 - 1896

EPILOGUE I

LAUSANNE 1937

Water is the best thing of all, and gold
Shines like flaming fire at night,
More than all a great man's wealth.
But if, my heart, you would speak
Of prizes won in the Games,
Look no more for another bright star
By day in the empty sky
More warming than the sun,
Nor shall we name any gathering
Greater than the Olympian.

OLYMPIAN I

Photo of Pierre de Coubertin one year before his death. He went to live in exile in Lausanne in Switzerland and never returned to France.

Comité International Olympique

Règlements
~~[établis le 23 juin 1894]~~

BUT — Le Comité International Olympique auquel le congrès International de Paris a confié la mission de veiller au développement des Jeux Olympiques solennellement rétablis le 23 Juin 1894 se propose 1°/ d'assurer la célébration régulière des Jeux — 2°/ de rendre cette célébration de plus en plus parfaite, digne de son glorieux passé et conforme aux idées élevées dont s'inspiraient ses rénovateurs — 3°/ de provoquer ou d'organiser toutes les manifestations et en général de prendre toutes les mesures propres à orienter l'athlétisme moderne dans les voies désirables.

EPILOGUE I

EPILOGUE I

LAUSANNE 1937

Pierre sat silently, waiting for Henri. It was a time of peaceful contemplation beside the lake. Some evenings there was no movement on the water. The moon grew fuller, reaching its half course, and seeming to swell from its crescent into a sphere as it changed colour. Before sunset it was white, almost diluted, but with the evening sky it became tinged with a rich yellow, and seemed to come lower when it had increased to practically its full size, touching the earth with a rich sensuous light. The still night and the lingering moon across the lake created a different atmosphere. The water was no longer so insistent, so remorseless. It seemed to pucker its surface very gently as the smallest wisp of breeze crossed its large still face, reposed in a delicate sleep. A soft, elegant murmer went down to its depths.

The ridge of the surrounding slopes could be seen better as the light from the moon increased. The slopes appeared engulfed in the lake as in strong protective arms while it lay there asleep, quite hushed and without movement. The moment between sunset and the full apparition of the moon was fragrant, delicious, and the most satisfying time of day. A life could be spent looking for such a light, such a view. It was the most mysterious beauty of all, the beauty of nature.

The moonlight over the lake was itself a perfect manifestation of memory, endlessly recurring but never the same. Yet it was different at each time, and even at different periods. The wood covered one slope in its protective cool greens. Nature had found a place in which to hide and weave out of its memory the fabric of a weightless dream. She could be trusted with constant regeneration.

The night was hung with stars. Occasionally one tumbled and then disappeared. In the immense silence of vast spaces, the stars were the sublime watchers of the earth, and by their fixed position, from their immense distance, the solitary traveller could chart his course, and guide himself after years of wandering to his true home. That home was the heart no longer full of longing for anywhere else, wrapped in the stillness of the night.

***

Henri sat in Pierre's study, overlooking Lake Geneva. There was a solemn expression on his face. Pierre seemed more feeble since the Berlin Games.

"What happened in Berlin, Henri?" said Pierre.

"All I remember was the large heavy doors of the Chancellor's office opening. When I entered, a second aide-de-camp, wearing white gloves, approached me. Hitler stood at the large window. We stayed still for a moment frozen in time. Hitler held his hands behind his back. A strip of light shot across his face. He turned slowly and his cold eyes met mine. Then I spoke.

"Herr Chancellor," I said, "the signs on the walls of the Olympic Stadium which say 'No Jews or Dogs', must be taken down immediately. Otherwise the International Olympic Committee will withdraw the Games from Berlin."

He looked at me coldly. Then he replied.

"The slogans of which your committee complain are placed there to protect the grounds from undesirable elements. It is a matter of internal German policy. I myself am fond of dogs, but they are not permitted, Mr. President Latour. You should understand that when you are invited to a friend's house, you do not tell him how to run it."

"What did you say?", said Pierre nervously.

I replied as calmly as possible.

"Excuse me, Mr. Chancellor. When the five-circled flag is raised over the Olympic stadium it is no longer Berlin, it is Olympia, and we are masters there."

Hitler did not reply. He turned once again towards the window. I felt a cold silence in the room. I learnt that the following day the signs were taken down."

Pierre listened to all of this. Henri was still in a visible state of shock. Even as he told the story, it was as if he couldn't believe it.

***

Henri had brought along a copy of Pierre's speech from Berlin. He was told that it had been listened to by a hushed audience of thousands.

Henri put on the recording. Pierre's words came crackling over the air...

"...courage was necessary to meet the difficulties which the Führer had encountered from the outset... in order to resist the disloyal and treacherous attacks from various quarters which sought to impede the advancing work of construction ... memories lastly of hope, for under the aegis of the five-ringed flag there has been forged understanding stronger than death itself."

"Freude, schoner Gotterfunken"

"Tochter aus..."

"the struggles of history will continue, but little by little knowledge will replace dangerous ignorance. Mutual understanding will soften unthinking hatred. Thus, the edifice at which I laboured at for half a century will be strengthened. May the German people and their head of state be thanked for what they have just accomplished! And you athletes, remember the sun-kindled fire, which has come to you from Olympia to lighten our epoch. Guard it jealously in the depths of your being!"

Henri switched off the recording with tears welling up in his eyes.

"I have to tell you something, Pierre."

"What is it, Henri?" asked Pierre, a little perturbed by Henri's reactions.

Henri paused a moment and looked out on the endless waters which stretched in the distance. He wished that he could delay this moment. He had not wanted to tell Pierre his real feelings about Berlin. He had held them back all these months.... the meaning of Berlin and the real truth behind the Games. He knew how the Games had been abused, how they had been made a vehicle of Nazi propaganda. It was as if a Greek goddess had been raped in front of thousands of lost souls. Henri had to tell him the truth, even if his dear old friend was possibly blinded by propaganda. Henri spoke.

"You have been tricked, Pierre. The Nazis tricked you."

"I realise that now, Henri, we should have withdrawn from Berlin," replied Pierre.

"It was impossible to know the extent of the abuse of the Jews."

"But we made a stand, Henri," replied Pierre, quite saddened now.

"It was not enough. We should not have listened to their ministers of propaganda. When you made that speech you were tricked by the Nazis."

"I know, Henri. At the time, I was promised that the Jews would be respected."

The room became silent. The two Olympic crusaders looked out on the waters of Lake Geneva, their figures illuminated by a flickering oil lamp.

But Pierre felt that he had made a stand at Berlin. The Nietzschean philosophy of 'the superman' adopted by the Nazis had been destroyed there. One black American, Jesse Owens, took Berlin by storm and proved that he was equal to the finest Germany could produce.

Pierre wondered, would the Olympics continue or would the symbol he had created be destroyed? Had the battle been lost at Berlin? Would the world forget what he had fought for? Perhaps the spirit would not live on. Would the world remember that the Olympics was a sacred ritual of peace? Pierre would suggest at the next meeting of the Olympic Committee that a truce be signed by all nations taking part. If a country infringed they would be banned at the next Olympics.

***

Pierre sat at his desk. It was the same one he had sat at in 1918.Since then he had written many letters and speeches to all corners of the world. Sometimes, as he scanned a phrase or a line, a touching memory or deep emotion was recalled. One speech struck a particular chord.

"The Olympic Games may be a potent, if indirect, factor in securing world peace. Wars break out because nations misunderstand each other. We shall not have peace until prejudices, which now separate the different races, are outlived. It is not visionary to look for similar benefactions in the future." He had been accused of being visionary and had replied in his defence. The world had criticised and despised visionaries, people who had led the way towards a new and better future.

He flicked through his papers and came across another speech.

"If I look back, I see from the end to the beginning my life as a man. I have been performing the job of a scout. A scout is one who goes forward to find the right way and the clear path. I was not aware of this occupation. I had chosen a different one and several times tried to escape it, always in vain. I think I was made for no other. At all events, an instinctive and secret force makes me stay faithful to it."

"However, it had its sorrows and setbacks. First of all, it implies solitude. There are hours when one feels terribly alone, as if lost in a dark forest or on a bare mountain top. At such moments one turns anxiously and longingly back. However, contact is found again. The scout returns to his tracks to impart his discovery, and check whether the crowd is indeed following in his footsteps. It is at that moment that he sometimes experiences keen disappointment. Yes, the crowd is following, but it has forgotten him. It credits others with the results of his labours, and he feels like a stranger amongst his fellows. His opinions are not listened to and his comments are not heeded. Disorientated and misunderstood, he starts to wish to be alone, and he goes off keener and more ambitious than ever, but with a painful sense of injustice in his heart."

Pierre felt this painful injustice once again. He had first experienced it in Athens, when the Greeks had tried to remove him from his position as reviver of the Games. He remembered that he was not even invited to the official enclosure. The Greek papers had called him a thief. Philemon, head of the Greek Olympic Committee, had written to him in February, 1896,

"The Hellenic Committee never credited to you the words, 'Founder of the Renaissance of the Olympic Games.'"

This had hurt him deeply at the time. It was only after the Games of 1896 that he made any declarations that he was the reviver of the Games. He came across a letter he had written on April 7th, just after the Games.

"The Games have often been criticised since then, and even violently attacked. Not everybody comprehends it; many speak of it without knowing anything about its origin or its purpose. As for myself, I hereby assert once more my claim to be the sole author of the entire project."

He realised that they had taken his beloved Games away from him in Berlin. They had used his name for propaganda. Even his old friend, Loues, had turned up in Berlin to present flowers of peace to Hitler. If only he could see his friend again! It was he who had inspired the world over forty years ago in Athens.

***

This painful sense of injustice returned to him again like an old wound. He had re-defined the course of history. He had spent his life in consultation with the makers of history, meeting presidents, kings, princes and ambassadors, in order to build his ideal. He had evoked the myths and spirits of the past. He knew, too, that history would judge him. What could he do to protect the Games? Was Berlin an omen of events to come? He gazed out upon the waters as the evening light faded rapidly and the moon appeared in the sky.

He looked into the heart of the past. He had followed the ideal. But had he expressed it sufficiently? Had he protected and strengthened it? Had he given it the shape and dimension it needed?

At the ancient hill, Kronion, situated in Olympia, the Olympics were created by the gods. Now he looked back to this myth, and this time with a sense of desperation. He had travelled a tortuous route. The sight of Olympia remained in his memory like a star which shone through the night. It was like a small star visible in the black night sky. It could guide the wanderer home.

As Henri got up to leave Pierre clasped his shoulders. He whispered,"Thank you, Henri… thank you! You have been a loyal friend."

It was a gesture that Pierre had never before shown to Henri. His aristocratic reserve had prohibited such displays of emotion. He now realised the true value of Henri's friendship. Henri had shown the deepest consideration for his feelings. Henri had fought bravely to preserve the Olympic ideal. Mistakes had been made at Berlin, but he had done his best to win a moral victory. Perhaps Henri had wished to give him a warning of what was to come. Even Churchill had indicated some months earlier that 'the dark cloud of fascism is descending over Europe.'

Henri's sense had been sharpened by experience. After all, he was Belgian. He had seen the devastation of his own country. He had seen the thousands of white crosses over the graves of unknown soldiers. Henri had been president of the Antwerp Games in 1926.

The Games were to be celebrated in Berlin in 1916, but were called off due to the Great War. Pierre had said 'that it was a bloody stain on the world's atlas.' He was relieved when the Games were held at Antwerp. He remembered the words of Aquinas, "Always be ready to struggle after each storm."

He had been through many storms and struggles in his own life. He had spent his entire fortune on the Games. In France he had been re-buffed. The ideas which he had started to develop there were not understood . He had witnessed the politeness of the establishment, the disenchanted civil servants. They had listened somewhat sceptically. He was never honoured in France in his own time. It was partly due to these factors that he had left France, forever, for final exile by the shores of Lake Geneva.

He had released his servants and sold his family home in 1918. This exile increased his isolation. The war had taken its toll on his family. His sister-in-law died when the Germans bombarded Paris. His two nephews were lost in combat on the battlefields which scarred the fields of France and Belgium. His son Jacques suffered from severe sunstroke at the age of two, only three years after the Athens Games, and was never to recover. His daughter also became unstable and required psychiatric care.

These tragedies ended the direct line of the de Coubertin family. His long lineage and its bloodline had come to an end. He had re-created a heritage for the world, but his own was dead.

He had been a rebel in his own way. He had created a revolution in his own lifetime. He was an idealist and a visionary. He had sacrificed all for a great dream, and had suffered the consequences.

He was forced to live in poverty for the last years of his life. His rooms at the chateau were donated by the civic authorities. He sought work but never found it. It was a friend, Dr. Messerli of Lausanne, who made an urgent appeal to the Olympic Committee for funds. This raised fifty thousand francs, but he refused money.

This created a strain between him and Marie. She had supported him faithfully in his great dream. Her devotion to Pierre remained unchanged until his death, but the events relating to their children filled them with grief.

Memories flashed through his mind like a flickering film at high speed: images, like sepia snapshots torn from an album. It was a ribbon of dreams that spanned one century to the next through two World Wars. There were memories of joy and deepest despair. He remembered his favourite lines, first heard in a London church in1908. That was the year his father died. It was also the year of the London Games. These were the words of an American bishop that would become the Olympic motto, "The important thing in life is not the triumph but the struggle; the essential thing is not to have conquered but to have fought well."

The Nazis had distorted Pierre's words at Berlin, on the giant Olympic screen that could be seen by all present in the stadium.

'The essential thing is not to have conquered but to have fought to win.,' they had changed his words. But it was not about winning, but the taking part. It was not about that 'Triumph of the will' which Leni Riefenstahl's film had celebrated. It was about 'the struggle' of each human being to attain their supreme potential.

Yet Pierre did indeed triumph by reviving the Olympic Games. He had waged a tremendous struggle with history. He won the battles against ignorance and stupidity. He had fought well against these forces, which attempted to destroy his enduring ideal.

Pierre watched the sun go up. At noon the midday sky was lazy, surrounded by a haze of heat. The notes from the first Congress lay on the table: the speech in which he first announced the Games. The letters were slightly tattered, but the writing was still absolutely legible. He had written that speech out several times and kept only the final copy. He read the words slowly:

"There are people who talk about the elimination of war; those who treat these people as Utopians are not wrong. But there are others who talk about the progressive diminution of the chances of war, and I don't see that as Utopian at all. What I mean is that on a basis conforming to modern life we are to establish a great and magnificent institution, the Olympic Games."

The Olympic idea had been the extraordinary discovery of the Greeks, a novelty in the mental life of that race. Everywhere else, cults based themselves on the hope for happiness beyond the tomb. For the Greeks it was present life which constituted happiness. Beyond the tomb there was only a diminished life, a partial survival.

The sun made its slow ascent as the high point of the day arrived. At the height of its course, it paled and then burnt most fiercely. Time stood still. The lake was completely placid. Violet and yellow streaks of light streamed across its surface. Fish swam around the little boats that were moored there. Small tinctures of blue and lavender flecked across the bobbing decks.

For Pierre now, his memories seemed shattered like a mirror.

His father had once created history on a canvas. Pierre's canvas now was filled with the great spectacle of people who attended the Games.

What could he recover from these fragments of memory? Hope had lingered on, even through all the tragedies. Pierre got up and lay on the chaise longue beside the French windows. Darkness was beginning to turn to an aquiline blue as night turned towards day. The waters of the lake became reflected in the blue of the early morning mist. He sat there, his silhouette illuminated in the light: a face that had weathered history with defiant nobility. He listened to some music on the gramophone. It was a section of Mahler's 5th symphony.

The events of the Franco-Prussian war of 1870 had, in a strange way, led him on his path to create an icon of hope in Europe. He recalled some words from Goethe which inspired him:

"The mist... is thus a fleeting darkness, and on the other side we will all find the sun and blue sky again."

Pierre's own words were influenced by Goethe's:

"The mist which is about to rise on your path, my dear young friends, is singular, opaque, dark and menacing. But never mind, plunge through the mist... you will find fresh sunlight and life on the other side. Courage, therefore, and hope. Indomitable courage and tenacious hope... strike boldly through the mist and have no fear, the future is with you."

The future, he knew, lay with the youth of the world to keep the flame burning. He remembered how he had given a speech addressed to the youth at Olympia in 1927.

"It is for you to keep the flag flying... Olympism is a school of moral nobility and purity."

He knew that he had succeeded and revived a great dream. But history had made him a forgotten hero.

His attempts at literary work had not achieved any success. His book on Universal History "Revolution Francaise" was not recognised by historians, or French intellectuals. His semi - autobiographical work "le Roman du rallie" did not achieve the success he had hoped for. Thus, his literary career had ended by 1900.

***

He listened now to the water's lapping. Mahler's music drifted across the lake. Towards the horizon the dawn light emerged. It lay there before him, the shimmering silvery waters of the lake like a thousand candles flickering in the darkness. He reflected upon the flame lit at Olympia. He imagined the bronzed athletes running forward in slow motion, like in a dream, with great power in their movements. He saw the cheering crowds. It was a memory, a vision that raced across the centuries, by heralds on their white horses blowing great heavenly trumpets announcing the past and the future. The gods of Olympia had, in a symbolic way, come to fight the Teutonic Knights at Berlin.

He reflected again. Words formed on his lips, the kind of words one finds solace from; words that he had once written and now brought tears to his eyes.

'Life is simple because the fight is simple. The good fighter steps forward, but never gives up. He yields but never quite quits. If he is faced with the impossible, he turns away and goes further... and even if everything falls down around him, despair does not enter him."

"Life is beautiful because the fight is beautiful. Not the bloody fight, fruit of tyranny and evil passions, which is maintained by ignorance and routine ... But the holy fight of souls seeking truth, light and justice."

***

Pierre looked out again upon the lake that now seemed to be covered in a silver mesh. It was like a floating silk sheet under the moonlight. This velvet curtain moved slowly in the cool evening breeze. His thoughts wandered again. Was there any point to his life now? He had hoped for so many things. He had not even been honoured in his own country. His achievement had been taken casually by the Government of the Third Republic. If only President Carnot had lived, he pondered.

A deep wave of sadness enveloped him. It is sometimes the tragedy of those who have done remarkable things to be judged as failures. These shattering events would not break him. What was it that had kept him sane during these last few years of poverty and depression? He knew instinctively what it was. His faith in his own beliefs had carried him on. That was the Olympic ideal.

He remembered that he had once said 'that the Olympic ideal was universal, and that no race or epoch can claim an exclusive monopoly to it.' Everything can be taken away from a man, but you cannot destroy his spirit. They had taken away his Olympic dream at Berlin, but its true spirit could not be destroyed. It was up to the youth of the future to continue what it stood for. Would they remember, or would the Olympic spirit die with him? Would the Olympics be abused again?

He thought of his dear friend Jules Simon who had once supported his dream. He found solace in his words, 'When climbing mountains, one must have a vision of joyful humanity.' Pierre had written about him,

"He had known difficulties, frustration and trouble. The difficulties of life were by no means spared him. Merited triumphs had eluded him."

Yet he recalled how Simon, even in his last years, had great hope and was filled with joy. Pierre compared Olympism to the Gospel when he wrote,

"Have faith in it. Put out your strength for it. Make its hopes your own."

All he could do now was hope and find solace in his own spirit, his own words and memories. He remembered Prague on May 29th, 1925. He had delivered a speech at the opening of the Olympic Congress. The words were an unwritten epitaph.

"When a man is going to leave his fruitful soil on which he has dwelt for many years, he will want, on his last day, to climb up to a high place whence he can see the horizon. There, musing on the future, he will worry over unfinished tasks. He will think of improvements which could be made and measured. None of you should be surprised that such should be my state of mind at the moment."

It was a state of mind that had remained for the last few years. What had he accomplished? What could he do to preserve the Olympic ideal? The sacred truce was, perhaps, the solution. This required that all wars should end when the Olympics began. Nine years after his speech in Prague, in 1934, Pierre was to write:

"Times are still difficult; the dawn which is breaking is that of the aftermath of the storm, but towards midday the sky will brighten and the ruddy corn will once more burden the arms of the harvester. It is not midday, gentlemen. The days of history are long; let us be patient and keep confident."

He knew that he had been blessed by favourable circumstances in his own life. He had been blessed by God in his quest. He wrote too of 'his struggle'.

"Perhaps one will judge that these remarks are inspired by pride. But if I have a high opinion of and take great pride in the work that was given to me to accomplish, I recognize no merit in it for myself. Merit begins there where the individual, obliged to struggle against himself or against excessively disfavorable circumstances, wins victories over his own temperament and, as it is said, succeeds in subduing his fate. Favored by lot in many respects, sustained unceasingly in the face of my task by a kind of internal force from which it happened that I searched in vain to escape, I count no such victories to my credit."

***

Pierre recalled again the King's speech at the great banquet at Athens. It was there that King George announced his desire that the Olympic Games be kept permanently at Athens. But Pierre's idea of the amateur code and the international principle remained with him. The Olympics should be moved around the world, he felt, changing the venue every four years.

It was an historical disagreement which would never be resolved. Vikelas tried to work out a compromise. He suggested a Greek Olympics every two years. Pierre remembered that he had reluctantly agreed. The Greeks had objected to plans for the holding of the Games in Paris in 1900. Pierre had given approval, with reservations.

Pierre succeeded Vikelas as President of the I.O.C. after the 1896 Games. Indeed, even now, Pierre recalled that this was the time where he pushed forward his Olympic dream. Sadly, it was then that his friendship with Vikelas had ended. Pierre looked at a letter he had found in his files from Vikelas. It was dated July 8th 1896.

'The Zappas Foundation did not re-establish the International Olympics; that credit is yours. But the fact remains that there have been in Greece Olympic Games, and that nobody could, even if they want, eradicate the name ... Nobody among us has the right to deny the name Olympics to the Athens Games.'

Pierre recalled that the Le Havre Conference in 1897 was critical. He had avoided placing the future of the Athens Games on this agenda. Vikelas never reached Le Havre that year, due to the death of his mother.

The I.O.C., however, agreed to award the Games to Athens in 1914. These would be the final Games for Vikelas; he died a year later. The dream for Athens Games was over.

***

Was there a future for the Olympics? Had they forgotten the essential truths of the ancient Games? Could its sacred truce be incorporated into the Olympic Charter, and ended conflict while the Games were on? Perhaps it could be extended to embrace the problems of racism, human rights and war. Could the I.O.C. refuse entry to countries who abused these issues? Was it too much to ask of the Games? Pierre pondered. It was open to debate.

Had he based the Games on the original ideals? In retrospect, not completely. The Games were not just about sport. It was an event originally where poets recited their verse and philosophers spoke of philosophy, where plays were performed and artists exhibited their sculpture and painting. Yes, he had not pursued this aspect of the Games, and he wondered could he organise for each country to send artists, poets, painters and philosophers to represent it. This would broaden the whole point of the Games. The emphasis on victory would be balanced towards participation in a broader cultural exchange.

What was required, even then? He realised that it was more than ever necessary to write it down succinctly and clearly, that no future Olympics should ever abuse the sacred truce; no future country could ever claim to send its representatives if they could not abide by the Olympic spirit and the sacred truce. They must agree to the cessation of all hostilities or, if they had taken part in a war with another country in the previous years before the Games, they would not be allowed to take part. They must observe the peace. If this was not observed, then everything was lost. He could see it clearly now, this truce that was a moral -~, the eternal, absolute ideal, as necessary and as important now as in ancient times. Pierre had become one of the first visionaries to regenerate an internationalism that would unite nations in the spirit of peace.

He had said that Olympism was a kind of religion not belonging to any era. It was essentially ecumenical in vision. The countries that took part should look towards cultural, political and ideological exchange. Thus, the Olympics would broaden its ideals and bring together many diverse cultures, with international exhibitions of Art, Theatre, Film and Literature from all over the world. In a world constantly beset by religious and political conflict, surely the direct contact with other cultures would allow individuals to understand other peoples. Yes, Pierre concluded, the Olympics did have a broader role to play in man's search for understanding.

Pierre remembered Goethe words,"Of all peoples, the Greeks have dreamt the dream of life best".

***

LAUSANNE 1937

Thedays of history are long,
let us be patient and
keep confident
De Coubertin

Gennadius Greek charge d'affaires London
A regular correspondent with Brookes and
the King of Greece.

Fr Didon
Friend and mentor of De Coubertin
and co-founder Comite des Exercises
Physiques.

Demetrius Vikelas
First President of the I.O.C

Athens Organising Committee and the I.O.C.
with Prince Constantine, Prine Nicholas and Prince George.

LAUSANNE 1937

The good fighter steps forward,
but never gives up.
De Coubertin.

Pierre's thoughts went out from his solitary abode in Lausanne. His mind drifted back to a sunlit afternoon forty years ago in Athens, 1896. It seemed only a short while had passed since then. He remembered that simple moment. The memories of all those years welled up in him, the feeling of total achievement. The wonder of the heroic ideal gripped him. The love and companionship he had experienced remained an indelible memory.

It was the name of a noble spirit calling out to him. He remembered the old tree he had planted on his visit to Dr. Brooke of Much Wenlock, out in the Olympian field. He was glad that time and nature had conspired in that faraway place to grant him the purpose of a life. His journey there had given him the most magical and unique direction. It was the interlocking of two existences, united by a common dream.

***

Pierre arose early one morning. He strolled in the park. Later he had breakfast on the veranda with Marie. He then retired to his study, as he always did, and read his endless correspondence. Sometimes he would leave the French windows open. Light would stream in through the panes, casting shadows across the room. He had begun entries into his diaries now. He compared his handwriting and how it had deteriorated over the last months. Berlin had receded into the past, and it seemed that his world had settled into an uneasy peace.

Unexpectedly, one morning, Marie entered with a flurry. Her cheeks were flushed, and she was out of breath.

"There's someone here to see you," she said, almost nervously.

"Who is it?" replied Pierre.

"Oh, my darling, you're not going to believe this. It's Loues. He is on his way back to Greece. He's come to see you."

Pierre suddenly raised his frail figure from the chair.

"Oh Loues, Loues! I haven't seen him since Athens. He disappeared into the mountains where we could never find him. Where is he?" replied Pierre excitedly.

Marie looked towards the doorway where the liquid light streamed in. Pierre's eyes followed hers. The figure of an old man appeared in the doorway. At first Pierre could not make out his stature, as the white light was too strong. Then the figure walked towards him, and the face of Loues appeared. Pierre looked at him in stunned silence.

"Oh Loues," he said with the deepest emotion, slowly embracing him.

Pierre held him by the shoulders, looking into his eyes. He examined the face of the old man, and tried to remember Athens."It's been so long," said Pierre, stretching his words.

"I always remember you," said Loues.

"How was Berlin?"

"You did not come. They promised me that I would see you."

"You gave flowers, and an olive wreath of peace to Hitler. It was such a mistake," replied Pierre, gripping his shoulders tightly.

"Hitler is not a good man," said Loues.

"They destroyed the Games, and abused everything that was

sacred to us," said Pierre.

"Nothing can destroy the Games," said Loues.

"I am sad, Loues, I am sad," said Pierre, casting his eyes to the floor.

"Don't be sad, my friend, they will never forget you. I have brought something for you," said Loues, returning through the sunlit door through which the light continued to stream. A moment later he entered again. In his hands he held the sacred cup of Olympia. Then he kissed it and handed it to Pierre.

"They tried to steal it from me in Berlin. I wanted you to have it back. The Games were your idea. Without you, there would have been nothing."

Pierre took the cup and a faint smile crept over his face. For a moment he remembered Dr. Brooke and that fateful day when he had set out on this quest fifty years before.

***

Loues stayed for some days with Pierre and Marie. They took walks down by the lake. It was an extraordinary meeting for them both. They had shared something quite wonderful in Athens together. Now, the final chapter in their lives was about to close.

The meeting brought feelings about Athens rushing back to Pierre. It was Loues that had made Athens a symbolic event. It was his achievement that had transcended the Games and made something immortal. Michael Breal had dreamed up the great idea, but Loues that had made it reality. He remembered now the moment of great elation, of the guns pounding across Athens and his arrival at the stadium. A great heroic moment in Greek history had come to life.

For one brief section of time the past merged with the present. Loues had become an immortal legend across Greece. Then he retired to his humble peasant life. He was never seen again on the world's stage, until Berlin.

However, Loues was not a forgotten hero. The Marathon and the Olympics were now inseparable; they were one. Of all the events in the Games, it was the Marathon which had a great myth behind it. It pitted man against nature, against great odds and against the elements.

Loues had remembered him! He was deeply touched that he had found his way to Geneva to see him and return the sacred cup. Pierre could now visualise the noble figure of Loues running down the last lap, with Constantine. In the great white marble stadium the crowds had cheered, and the King of Greece held up the gleaming cup to the victor.

Pierre sat back in his chair and took the cup into his hands. It was this cup that had set him out on his journey forty years before! It was this cup that had given purpose to his life! All the trapped emotions of the Games welled up inside him. The cup had given him his ideal, and he honoured this victorious man who had returned once again to see him.

Saying good-bye to Loues was a painful experience. He knew instinctively that he would never see him again. Loues had brought back the memories of Athens to him in a great flash of emotion. Of all the events and moments of the preceding Games, none could match Loues's achievement. He had ran a race not run for over a thousand years. He had achieved the impossible and made history. When Loues left him, Pierre knew that one of the most important friends in his life had gone forever.

***

SEPTEMBER 2 1937

The Olympic Games may be apotent ,if indirect factor
in securing world peace.
De Coubertin.

Loues forthy years after the Athens Games is invited to the Berlin Games and presents Hitler with a laurel wreath of peace.

Marie de Coubertin 1859-1963

Pierre began to take walks by the lake, where he pondered his thoughts. It was here Byron and Shelly had walked together on the shores of this very lake, before Byron had set out on his final journey to Greece. Pierre knew that he would make this final journey soon.

He continued to walk daily across Parc Le Grange. He could no longer go out rowing. His limbs weren't quite up to it. The slow walk invigorated him as he crossed the park in his white flannel suit. A cool breeze wafted over him. The early morning sun created a shimmering surface on the lake. It was as if thousands of lights were suspended there.

His thoughts continued to revolve around the past. He looked back to the civilization of ancient Greece and remembered Olympia. He was re-united with great and noble gods, that raced in chariots across the centuries. They beckoned him to recreate and to show the world the nobility and glory of ancient Greece and remembered Olympia. He was re-united with great and noble gods, that raced in chariots across the centuries. They beckoned him to recreate and to show the world the nobility and glory of ancient Greece, with its ancient power as the fountain of all ideas. A dormant seed lay beneath the ruins of its temples: a civilization long dead, but living in the imagination.

There was something in the human psyche, deeply embedded in the unconscious, that he desperately wanted to appeal to. It was the element of sacred truths, of noble actions, of heroic deeds in creating a finer man. He wanted to appeal to the human spirit that was in essence heroic.

The ancient bronzed runner had crossed endless time. He carried the spirit of Olympia. It was a code of ethics that man could live by. The heroic spirit belonged to the great myths, and Pierre had used these myths to inspire the world. That was the secret of the

Olympics.

He had harnessed one of the great symbols of human history. It was similar to the symbol of the Crucifixion and the ascent into Heaven; the fight between the devils and the angels at Armageddon. Myths had a power all of their own. Pierre had appealed to the heroic imagination. He had moved men to recreate a great and noble past.

***

Pierre now passed beneath the oak trees in the park that sheltered him from the strong midday sun. He felt a little tired from his walk along the lake. Perspiration covered his brow. His plan, every day, was to reach the furthest point in the park and return again. But this time he felt that the distance was a long one. He looked across the lake and observed the shimmering light, dancing across the waters.

For a moment a figure appeared, a figure of a young girl with long tapering wings motioning against the waters of the lake. It was Nike, the Goddess of Victory. The figure slowly waved its hand as if to wave good bye; then the image melted in the shimmering surface of the lake. Then Pierre's eyes swung up towards the sun. For a moment it seemed as if the great flame filled his vision.

Then the pain came almost in a flash: an intense sharp pain that shot up from the base of his elbow, along his right arm and into his chest. It was like an arrow, moving with great velocity. The pain was intense. It seemed as if his heart was a burning fire. For a moment, a split second, he thought of Marie. Then he collapsed to the ground.

***

It was more than an hour later that one of the servants found his body. Marie was soon by his side, filled with a deep sadness, realising that it was not just her loss, but also the world's.

Marie sat on the veranda that evening. She had not stopped crying for some hours. Her friend Madeleine consoled her, caressing her forehead and holding her hand. All the memories of Pierre flooded back to her ... memories of their life together... memories of love, and images of the games.

Then she remembered that Pierre had left her a will in the safe behind the print of Le Grand Odalisque. In the study Marie found the key in Pierre's desk. She hurried downstairs with her lamp. In the glowing light Marie opened the letter and studied the lines:

"My dear Marie,

"Please do not be saddened by my death. My spirit is with you always. Forgive me for not leaving you anything of value. Some people choose a path to serve others. This was my path. I think there could have been no other way. Perhaps it was foolish of me, spending all my money on my great project. There is one last request that I would make of you; bury my body in Lausanne, but take my heart first from my body, so that it may be buried at Olympia. That is where my heart has always been and should be at rest.

'I will be with you always, Marie.

"All my love,

"Pierre."

He would return to Olympia; his heart would be buried there.

Not lodged in his body, but out there, under a blue sky, in a beautiful wooded valley. But though he was dead, Marie understood that his spirit could not rest until the world remembered the truth of his most profound symbol.

***

Henri Latour heard the news at his house in Brussels later that night. At first he could not quite believe the shattering news. Somehow he thought that his friend Pierre would live on into his nineties, immortal like a Greek god. It was as if he had been claimed too early by the ranks of death.

It was a solemn moment for Henri because he felt that a new era was over and now the great mentor of the Games was dead.

Who would now carry the torch and the ideal? He left Brussels that night and travelled overnight to Lausanne. Marie greeted him and he consoled her. She told him of Pierre's last request and asked his advice. Pierre, even in death, was creating symbols, one great final moment that summed up the totality of his life's work. Olympia was where the ideal had begun. It was where the flame had been re-kindled. Now his heart was to be placed beneath a white marble column.

Some days later, they attended Pierre's funeral in the cemetery of Bois de Vaux in Lausanne. Pierre's heart had been cut from his body and placed in a satin-lined golden casket. Early one morning this casket was presented to Henri and Marie by the local chaplain. Tears welled in Marie's eyes as she kissed the golden casket and laid it upon the table.

It would be some months before Henri could carry out Pierre's final request. There was a flurry of diplomatic activity between Lausanne, Brussels and Athens. There were no objections, how ever, from the Greek government or the royal family. In Athens a white marble column, not unlike an obelisk, was inscribed, 'To the memory of the renovator of the Olympics.'

***

EPILOGUE II

When, to their airy hall, my fathers' voice
Shall call my spirit, joyful in their choice:
When, pois'd upon the gale, my form shall ride,
Or, dark in mist, descend the mountain's side;
Oh! may my shade behold no sculptur'd urns,
To mark the spot where earth to earth returns:
No lengthen'd scroll, no praise encumber'd stone;
My epitaph shall be my name alone:
If that with honour fail to crown my clay,
Oh! may no other fame my deeds repay;
That, only that, shall single out the spot;
By that remember'd, or with that forgot.

BYRON. A FRAGMENT.

LAUSANNE: OLYMPIA 1938

In the middle of March 1938, Henri Latour made a final journey to Olympia. He carried the golden casket, safely protected in a wooden box, across Europe. It was a solemn journey for Henri; somehow he felt that the spirit of Pierre travelled late into the night with him as the train rattled down through Europe.

Henri travelled alone with the casket; he was informed, however, that a number of dignitaries would attend the funeral service at Olympia. He leaned out of the window and said good-bye to Marie. She stood alone on the platform. He could see there was sadness in her eyes with the realisation that Pierre was gone forever. Henri felt the pain too, welling up inside of him.

The wind blew in his face. The train, gathering speed, headed out of Lausanne, and travelled through Zurich, then on to Innsbruck. Over an hour later it stopped near the Yugoslavian border, at the town of Villach. Henri's thoughts revolved around Pierre ; memories floated through his mind of Pierre's conversations, of his dreams, of his never ending passion. Now he was gone! What remained was his heart, and one final symbol that was to be erected at Olympia.

The train sped on through the night to Zagreb, but Henri could not sleep. The conductor offered him some tea, but he felt restless. Sometimes he would place his hand on the wooden box, holding the casket. He was filled with sadness, with a feeling of overwhelming loss. The faint light of the rising sun gleamed across the landscape. Henri fell asleep.

After Sarajevo the train took up speed again. It headed south through the mountains towards Greece. He could smell the olives in the air, and the sweet fragrances of Greece, as they approached the border. The Greek sun shone down relentlessly across the early morning landscape. Henri spotted a shepherd gathering his sheep from the hillside. He glimpsed a fallen temple.

At Saloniki he observed the pale blue Ionian sea. The train wound its way along the Greek coastline. He imagined he saw the reflection of Pierre in the window, smiling at him. Was it a trick of the light or some ghostly reassurance from Pierre, that Henri was carrying out his final wish? He was tired and could not tell. He did not want to analyse this strange vision. Perhaps the memory of his dear friend was so fixed in his mind that he had conjured it up from the depths of his imagination.

Temples gleamed in the sun. The ancient Acropolis hung over Athens, nobly defying the future, reminding its citizens of their ancient past. Henri breathed a sigh of relief. Athens at last!

OLYMPIA

At Olympia on March 26th, 1938, an extraordinary ceremony took place. Crown Prince Paul, the grandson of Prince Constantine, arrived in military dress. Count Berthier de Sauvigny, member of the International Olympic Committee, and Pierre's old comrade, Count Alexandre Mercati, member of the I.O.C. and Monsieur C. Georgopoulos, the Greek Minister of Public Worship, were present. Count Berthier gave a brief address.

"We come here today to pay our last respects to our dear friend, Pierre de Coubertin. No man has done so much this century for the creation of international co-operation and peace. Yet his name and work has not been honoured even in his own country. L et us pray that he will be remembered, and that his contribution to world peace will be understood. Let us hope that it will be continued in the spirit he created."

A Greek Orthodox priest stepped forward with two altar boys, shaking their incense bowls. The priest was dressed in the finest costume of gold and red. He read from an ancient bible.

"Blessed are the meek. Blessed are the seekers of peace, for they shall inherit the earth."

Then the priest blessed the casket, which was placed beneath the marble column; and Pierre's heart rested where his spirit had always been.

***

For Pierre a final symbol was erected: a marble obelisk to mark the place. Not unlike the grave of his uncle. An unquiet soul that had waited for decades for one human voice to come and release him from the dead. He had once knelt at his uncle's grave and made a promise to build another symbol. Now Pierre had created his final symbol.

Would he too, be forgotten like his uncle? Would those who continued his sacred Games remember him and his ideas? He had restored his uncle's name to his family history. He had put an unquiet soul to rest. He had resurrected the soul and the spirit of Olympia that had lain dormant for over fifteen hundred years. He had moved the hearts and minds of men to achieve his ideal.

This one final symbol summed up his life's work. He was buried close to the altar where the flame was lit. He would always be close to the golden flame; golden because it was everlasting, golden because it was eternal, because it stood for peace and symbolized hope. His hope was that it would burn forever.

This ideal had consumed him as he sat alone on the shores of Lake Geneva and awaited the final journey. At Olympia he had rekindled the golden flame. His will had directed that his heart be buried there, buried in a golden casket with a simple inscription. He understood that whatever the events in his life had been, to fight alone was his destiny. This was the path he had taken.

But, paradoxically, it was a meeting with a small, white-whiskered country doctor that had begun his quest. It was in England that he had discovered Greece. It was there he learnt of Olympia and found the ideal of his life.

In a small Shropshire village he had found the calm love of the rarest of all human beings, a simple old man with a dream to relight the flame of Olympia. A simple old man who loved him as a son, who had given him an ideal. He had given him this love, an ideal, a sacred truth. lie had given to him the meaning of his life. From that village, from that wonderful old man, he had found his way to Olympia.

***

At Olympia on March 26th, 1938, an extraordinary ceremony took place. Crown Prince Paul, the grandson of Prince Constantine, arrived in military dress. Count Berthier de Sauvigny, member of the International Olympic Committee, and Pierre's old comrade, Count Alexandre Mercati, member of the I.O.C. and Monsieur C. Georgopoulos, the Greek Minister of Public Worship, were present.

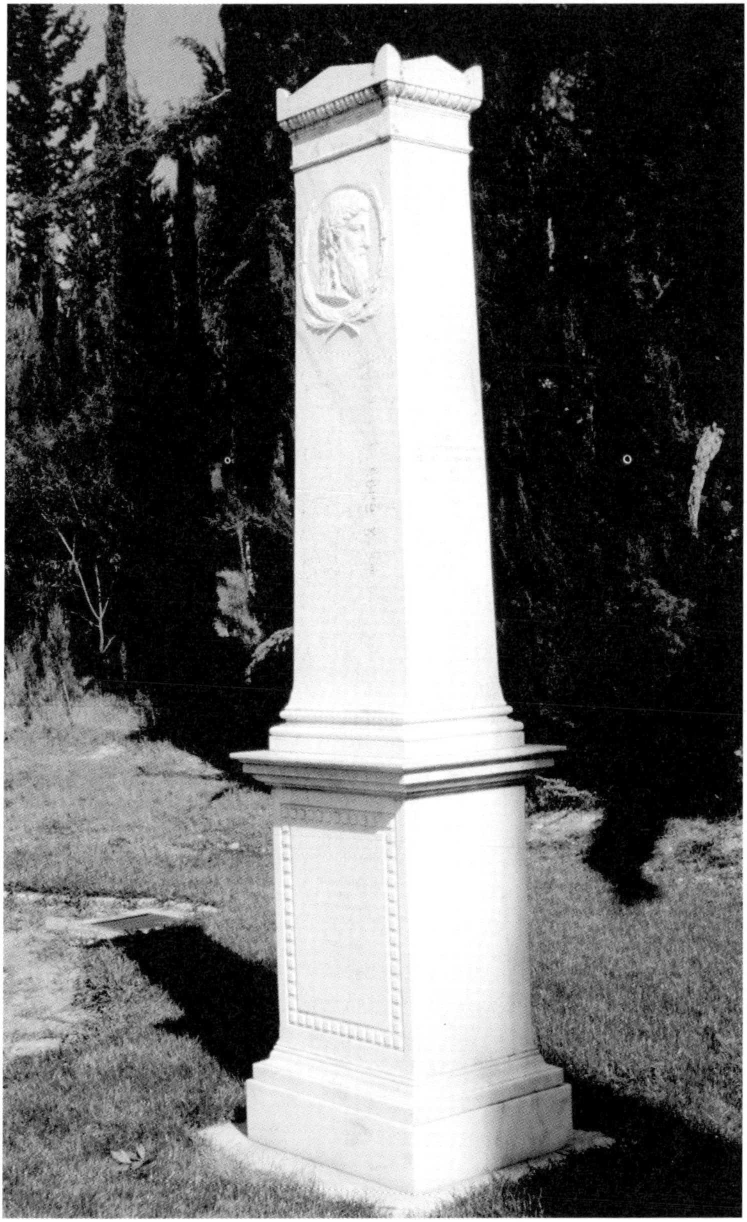

In 1925 Pierre de Coubertin resigned from the International Olympic Committee. His final words on the movement were:

"Gentleman at this hour I put you on guard against sports professionalism. The organisers of societies tends to corrupt the athletes, to better satisfy the spectator."

From de Coubertin's resignation speech 1925.

" It is necessary to recall that Olympism cannot be manipulated by any particular group. They are world wide. All people should be admitted
without discussion. As well as all sports should be treated on an equal footing."

De Coubertin's speech. Prague 1925.

PICTURE CREDITS

Library of Congress: .Olympia-Film: Library of Congress: Press Sports: M.: B.O.A:. I.O.C. Archives:Brown Bros. :Hellenic Association: Hellenic Association.I.O.C Archives: Library of Congress.Hellenic Association:
Brown Bros: Trinity College: Caliver Pictures: 33. Olympia Film: 34 Much Wenlock Museum:Athens Library: B. O. A.: Historical Picture Service.
Benaki Musuem.National Historical Musuem.

QUOTATIONS

Chapter headings. Pindar's ode's. Penguin edition. Byron's poems:
Oxford University Press.

AKNOWLEDGEMENTS

I.O.C. Library, Lausanne. British Olympic Association.U.K. .Library of Congress, U.S.A. Sorbonne..Paris. Harvard Library. Trinity Library.Dublin.
The Much Wenlock Olympian Society. Mr John Sympson. Norman Wood.Helen Cromary, Glyn Mc Donald. Aida Wild, Patrick Healy, John Menehann, Alistar Greene, Maria Elena Doyle, Theo Primus, Corrine Quentin, James Hawkridge, Greta Baars Jelgersmana Demetrious Cristou, Michael Youlton, Lord Killanin.Natalie Jones. Don Mc Guinness.Roy Eagle. Libby Jones. Colon O Colmain.Joan Bazouki. Tony Centurion. Nicola Pool. Baron Geoffrey de Navacelles .Catherine Chapius, David Ollier.Constantine de Naray.Alexander Spentzos.
Special thanks to the following who without their Olympian efforts this book would not have been produced.Cormac Crawford..KristinaLynn.ClaudiaWalker.RegEagle.Jayne Gaskin Paul White.Heike.Stephen StreetLRPS.Nicola Poole.Heike Conors.

ΟΛΥΜΠΙΑ[Η]
ΑΓΩΝΕΣ

JEUX OLYMPIQUES

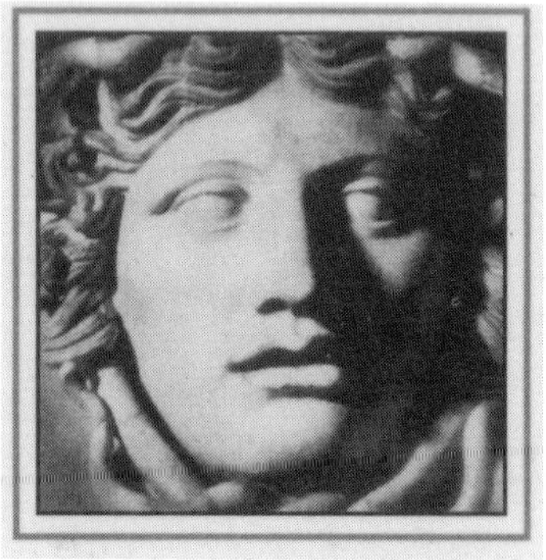

The Golden Flame gives an accurate account account and heroic vision and ethos of the founders of the modern Olympics.
Cormac A Crawford
Former commercial advisor to the Olympic Council of Ireland
Barcelona and Atlanta Olympic Games.

A story of a great endeavour
Lord David Puttnam M.P.
Producer of Chariots of Fire

A beautiful book
Helen Cromarty
Much Wenlock Olympian Society

The most extradonary day of my life was the day I tried to prevent the boycott of the Moscow Games.
I sat with Breznev in the Kremlin ,then took a flight to Washington to meet with President Carter at the White house.
The Golden Flame explores similar battles that I and De Coubertin fought for.
Lord Killanin
President of the International Olympic Committee 1972-1980

A book of extraordinary detail.
John Bryant
Deputy Editor of The Times.

The only Phil ñHellenic novel written by an Irish author since Joyces Ulysses
Patrick Healy .Joycean Scholar.Author of the Modern and the Wake.

Murray knows more about history than us Greeks.
Alexander Spentzos.Film Distributor.Producer.
Spentzos Films S.A. Athens.

The Golden Flame perfectly captures the personality , philosophy
and character of Pierre De Coubertins life.
Baron Geoffery(De Coubertin) De Navacalle
Grand nephew of Pierre De Coubertin.
Former chairman of the International De Coubeertin Committee.

The only book mainstream on the Athens Games
Thanos
Chairman of Efstathiadis Group S.A.

The dream the struggle the triumph ñfiction and reality at its best.
James Meehan
Standard Newspaper

The book has all the colour and exitement of an epic journey .The symbol of the Marathon which pitted man against nature and the elements makes it a story that convinces the reader that he is sparticipating in the human race for excellence.A challenge to us all but especially to the young.
Anne Sherrerd Murphy
Kilkenny People.Review.

Gabriel is immersed in the arts.
Sean Keane
Editor of the Kilkenny People.

A book that re captures the heroic struggles of De Coubertin and the great battle that he sacraficed everything for.
Prince Fredrick von Saxe Laurenberg.
Former member of the International De Coubertin Committee.

An epic story
Constantine Denaray
Film producer ; The Young Alexander the Great

A wonderful book that will make an Oscar winning film
Joseph Drier
Director of Hollywood Classics.

A great read
Noel Pearson
Producer of My Left Foot